OPPOSING
VIEWPOINTS®
SERIES

Paranormal
Phenomena

Other Books of Related Interest

Opposing Viewpoints Series

Cults

At Issue Series

Should Religious Symbols Be Allowed on Public Land?

Current Controversies Series

Espionage and Intelligence

"Congress shall make no law … abridging the freedom of speech, or of the press."

First Amendment to the US Constitution

The basic foundation of our democracy is the First Amendment guarantee of freedom of expression. The Opposing Viewpoints Series is dedicated to the concept of this basic freedom and the idea that it is more important to practice it than to enshrine it.

Paranormal
Phenomena

Roman Espejo, Book Editor

GREENHAVEN PRESS
A part of Gale, Cengage Learning

Detroit • New York • San Francisco • New Haven, Conn • Waterville, Maine • London

Elizabeth Des Chenes, *Director, Publishing Solutions*

© 2013 Greenhaven Press, a part of Gale, Cengage Learning

Gale and Greenhaven Press are registered trademarks used herein under license.

For more information, contact:
Greenhaven Press
27500 Drake Rd.
Farmington Hills, MI 48331-3535
Or you can visit our Internet site at gale.cengage.com.

Cover image © Design Pics/Don Hammond/Getty Images.

LIBRARY OF CONGRESS CATALOGING-IN-PUBLICATION DATA

Paranormal phenomena / Roman Espejo, book editor.
    pages cm. -- (Opposing viewpoints)
    Includes bibliographical references and index.
    ISBN 978-0-7377-6334-8 (hardcover) -- ISBN 978-0-7377-6335-5 (pbk.)
    1. Parapsychology. I. Espejo, Roman, 1977-
    BF1031.P3343 2013
    130--dc23

                        2012036909

Printed in the United States of America
1 2 3 4 5   17 16 15 14 13

Contents

Chapter 3: Are Paranormal Investigations and Practices Legitimate?

Why Consider
Opposing Viewpoints?

*"The only way in which a human being
can make some approach to knowing
the whole of a subject is by hearing
what can be said about it by persons of
every variety of opinion and studying
all modes in which it can be looked at
by every character of mind. No wise
man ever acquired his wisdom in any
mode but this."*

John Stuart Mill

In our media-intensive culture it is not difficult to find differing opinions. Thousands of newspapers and magazines and dozens of radio and television talk shows resound with differing points of view. The difficulty lies in deciding which opinion to agree with and which "experts" seem the most credible. The more inundated we become with differing opinions and claims, the more essential it is to hone critical reading and thinking skills to evaluate these ideas. Opposing Viewpoints books address this problem directly by presenting stimulating debates that can be used to enhance and teach these skills. The varied opinions contained in each book examine many different aspects of a single issue. While examining these conveniently edited opposing views, readers can develop critical thinking skills such as the ability to compare and contrast authors' credibility, facts, argumentation styles, use of persuasive techniques, and other stylistic tools. In short, the Opposing Viewpoints Series is an ideal way to attain the higher-level thinking and reading skills so essential in a culture of diverse and contradictory opinions.

In addition to providing a tool for critical thinking, Opposing Viewpoints books challenge readers to question their own strongly held opinions and assumptions. Most people form their opinions on the basis of upbringing, peer pressure, and personal, cultural, or professional bias. By reading carefully balanced opposing views, readers must directly confront new ideas as well as the opinions of those with whom they disagree. This is not to argue simplistically that everyone who reads opposing views will—or should—change his or her opinion. Instead, the series enhances readers' understanding of their own views by encouraging confrontation with opposing ideas. Careful examination of others' views can lead to the readers' understanding of the logical inconsistencies in their own opinions, perspective on why they hold an opinion, and the consideration of the possibility that their opinion requires further evaluation.

Evaluating Other Opinions

To ensure that this type of examination occurs, Opposing Viewpoints books present all types of opinions. Prominent spokespeople on different sides of each issue as well as well-known professionals from many disciplines challenge the reader. An additional goal of the series is to provide a forum for other, less known, or even unpopular viewpoints. The opinion of an ordinary person who has had to make the decision to cut off life support from a terminally ill relative, for example, may be just as valuable and provide just as much insight as a medical ethicist's professional opinion. The editors have two additional purposes in including these less known views. One, the editors encourage readers to respect others' opinions—even when not enhanced by professional credibility. It is only by reading or listening to and objectively evaluating others' ideas that one can determine whether they are worthy of consideration. Two, the inclusion of such viewpoints encourages the important critical thinking skill of objectively evaluating an author's credentials and bias. This evaluation will illuminate an author's reasons for taking a particular stance on an issue and will aid in readers' evaluation of the author's ideas.

It is our hope that these books will give readers a deeper understanding of the issues debated and an appreciation of the complexity of even seemingly simple issues when good and honest people disagree. This awareness is particularly important in a democratic society such as ours in which people enter into public debate to determine the common good. Those with whom one disagrees should not be regarded as enemies but rather as people whose views deserve careful examination and may shed light on one's own.

Thomas Jefferson once said that "difference of opinion leads to inquiry, and inquiry to truth." Jefferson, a broadly educated man, argued that "if a nation expects to be ignorant and free . . . it expects what never was and never will be." As individuals and as a nation, it is imperative that we consider the opinions of others and examine them with skill and discernment. The Opposing Viewpoints Series is intended to help readers achieve this goal.

David L. Bender and Bruno Leone,
Founders

Introduction

> "Altogether, scientific evidence suggests that all features of the near-death experience have some basis in normal brain function gone awry."
>
> Charles Q. Choi, science journalist

> "No skeptic, medical or otherwise, has ever investigated the entire phenomenon—the near-death experience and its aftereffects—to any appreciable degree or with a research base large enough for informed comment."
>
> P.M.H. Atwater, author of Near-Death Experiences, The Rest of the Story: What They Teach Us About Living and Dying and Our True Purpose

Before she died in May 2010, Pam Reynolds Lowery purportedly had a near-death experience nineteen years earlier that made paranormal history. In Arizona, the singer-songwriter from Georgia was on the operating table—her eyes taped shut, her ears fitted with molded speakers—for the removal of a brain aneurysm. Doctors reduced her body temperature to 60 degrees and induced a "cardiac standstill," stopping her heart. During surgery, Reynolds Lowery said she "popped" out of her head and floated above the table, seeing people around her body and a tool that looked like her electric toothbrush. She also heard the song

"Hotel California" in the room. "I realized it was my body, but I felt less attached to it than to some cars I've had to get rid of," Reynolds Lowery told the *Atlanta Journal-Constitution*. Going down a tunnel vortex with a light at the end, she met her deceased uncle and grandmother, who urged her to turn around and accompanied her back to the operation.

A year later, assuming that these details were hallucinations, Reynolds Lowery shared them with her brain surgeon, Robert Spetzler. To his astonishment, they matched what he remembered. "From a scientific perspective, I have absolutely no explanation about how it could have happened," he says. Cardiologist and researcher Michael Sabom compared her testimony to medical records of the surgery. "Long story short, what she said happened to her is actually what Spetzler did with her out in Arizona," insists Sabom, reiterating that she could not see or hear during the operation.

Reynolds Lowery's story has become one of the most famous and renowned near-death experiences. Kenneth Ring, professor emeritus of psychology at the University of Connecticut, declares hers as "the single best instance we now have in the literature on near-death experiences to confound the skeptics," with documentation and corroboration from medical professionals. The paranormal phenomenon is reported to have happened to 15 percent of Americans who nearly died, according to the 1982 book *Adventures in Immortality* by George Gallup. Of this group, 9 percent had out-of-body experiences; 11 percent went to heaven, hell, or other realms; and 8 percent encountered spiritual entities. In addition, Ring describes several lasting impacts of near-death-experiences, including a greater sense of purpose in life, lesser fear of death, and stronger religious feelings. William "Butch" Lowery, who was married to Reynolds Lowery, claims that his wife became more compassionate after her near-death experience. "She could be standing in line at a grocery store and detect people there who were troubled, some of them so much so that it could move her to tears," he explains.

Some of the most recent evidence for near-death experiences comes from Jeffrey Long, a radiation oncologist and author of *Evidence of the Afterlife: The Science of Near-Death Experiences*, which was published in 2010. Having studied about 1,300 near-death experiences, he contends that its main characteristics—as seen in Reynold Lowery's account—transcend age and cultures, consistently bearing similarities in ways that defy easy explanation. "I think if near-death experiences were culturally determined, then people that had never heard of near-death experiences would have a different experience," Long said in an interview on the *Today* show. "But we're not finding that." He maintains that children ages five and younger in his research had the same experiences as older individuals—despite not fully grasping the meaning of death. "It suggests that whether you know about near-death experiences, what your cultural upbringing is, what your awareness of death is, it doesn't seem to have any effect on the content of the near-death experience," Long asserts. Furthermore, the blind—even those born that way—can have "fully visual impressions during their near-death experiences just like visual impressions during other near-death experiences."

Numerous researchers, however, state that near-death experiences are caused by physiological processes that occur when dying. Kevin Nelson, a neurologist and author of *The Spiritual Doorway in the Brain: A Neurologist's Search for the God Experience*, proposes that the tunnel and light are simple to explain. "When this happens, the eye fails before the brain fails. The outside field of vision goes first, but the center is preserved until the very end, so you develop a tunnel-like sensation," Nelson claims. "As for the light, when your eye loses blood flow, light might become all that you're capable of seeing." It is also suggested that this feature of near-death experiences—as well as leaving the body and spiritual visions—can be attributed to intense brain activity that happens at the time. "We think the near-death experiences could be caused by a surge of electrical energy released as the brain runs out of oxygen," claims Lakhmir Chawla, associate professor of medicine at George Washington University Medical Center. "As blood flow slows down and oxygen levels fall, the brain cells fire one last electrical impulse. It starts in one part of the brain and spreads in a cascade, and this may give people vivid mental sensations."

As for Reynolds Lowery recalling the specifics of her brain surgery, anesthesiologist and researcher Gerald Woerlee persists that there is nothing paranormal about it. "There are various explanations," he argues. "One: that the earphones or plugs were not that tightly fitting. Two: It could have been that it was due to sound transmission through the operating table itself." Woerlee also alleges that her tool description was drawn from past memories and she had anesthesia awareness; Reynolds Lowery was conscious, but paralyzed during the operation.

The near-death experience is one of several types of paranormal phenomena. From ghost hunters on television to psychic detectives on crime scenes, the supernatural—although unproven and unsupported by mainstream science—is a part of US culture. *Opposing Viewpoints: Paranormal Phenomena* examines paranormal topics in the following chapters: Do Paranormal Phenomena Exist?, Why Do People Believe in Paranormal Phenomena?, and Are Paranormal Investigations and Practices Legitimate? The varying perspectives presented in this volume embody the curiosity, conviction, and skepticism evoked by the unexplained.

OPPOSING
VIEWPOINTS®
SERIES

CHAPTER 1

Do Paranormal Phenomena Exist?

Chapter Preface

William of Occam, a medieval English logician and friar, declared that "entities should not be multiplied unnecessarily." Today, his statement is the foundation of Occam's Razor, a principle stating that "when you have two competing theories that make exactly the same predictions, the simpler one is the better." Prominent Austrian physicist Ernst Mach promoted his understanding of Occam's Razor in scientific study and experimentation in the nineteenth century. "Scientists must use the simplest means of arriving at their results and exclude everything not perceived by the senses," Mach stated.

Skeptics have adopted the principle to challenge proof of paranormal phenomenon. "Occam can be applied to a myriad of supposed paranormal events, including ghosts, psychics, UFOs, people who talk with the dead, reincarnation, the soul, spoon benders, near death, and out-of-body experiences," says Richard Rockley, who runs the blog *Skeptico*. "Usually, the paranormal explanation for these phenomena cannot be disproven, and this is often given as the reason we should consider the paranormal explanation. But Occam says go with the natural explanation for now, until any new evidence challenges it."

In dissent, paranormal investigators claim that the reasoning of Occam's Razor is flawed. "This argument is a principle that skeptics often misuse to try to force alternate explanations to paranormal ones, even if those explanations involve false accusations or do not fit the facts," maintains the Scientific Committee to Evaluate PseudoSkeptical Criticism of the Paranormal (SCEPCOP) on its website. SCEPCOP points out that the simpler explanation is not always correct, and skeptics even go so far as to accept or invent overly complicated ones— as long as it does not support paranormal activity. "Skeptics treat Occam's Razor as if it were an absolute rule and use it as a label for denying any paranormal claim, no matter how valid," the committee insists. Authors in the following chapter attempt to debunk or validate evidence of paranormal activity.

> *"Even if a highly credible source with a long history of accuracy suddenly makes a paranormal claim or a claim against an established view, they automatically dismiss it as bunk."*

Skeptics Ignore Evidence for Paranormal Phenomena

Winston Wu

In the following viewpoint, a paranormal researcher argues that legitimate evidence for paranormal phenomena is dismissed by skeptics and the scientific community. According to the author, controlled scientific experiments and credible anecdotal sources support the existence of various paranormal phenomena, but skeptics deny any evidence that does not fit into their views and scientists continue to stigmatize the field. The author maintains that skeptics routinely demand evidence just to ignore it, indicating a bias against the paranormal. Winston Wu is the founder of the Scientific Committee to Evaluate PseudoSkeptical Criticism of the Paranormal (SCEPCOP) and author of Debunking Pseudo-Skeptical Arguments of Paranormal Debunkers.

As you read, consider the following questions:

1. What happens to scientists who support the legitimacy of paranormal phenomena, according to Wu?
2. In Wu's opinion, why are skeptics deluded and not facing reality?
3. How do skeptics treat controlled experiments demonstrating psychic ability, according to Wu?

Pseudoskeptics are always saying, "There's no evidence for any paranormal or psychic phenomena" no matter how much evidence is shown to them. That's because this statement is a religion to them, not an objective statement. So no matter what evidence you give them, they will always deny it and raise the bar, simply because "there is no evidence" is a fixed belief to them.

So, if you give them stories and experiences, even from credible sources, they will reject it as "anecdotal" and inadmissible as evidence. If you give them scientific studies that show positive results for psi [parapsychology], they will argue that those studies did not have proper controls (since, if they did, they'd only get chance results, so their fixed logic goes). And they will argue that the studies must be replicable. Then when you show them replicated studies, they will raise the bar again and argue it was not replicated enough times (until a debunker disproves it is what they mean), ad infinitum. So no matter how many stories or replicable research studies you cite, it's NEVER enough. There is no clear bar to meet to qualify as "real evidence" to them, because essentially, there is NO EVIDENCE in their mind, thus there is no real criteria to be met. That gives them the license to deny ad infinitum. It's like playing a shady game of three shells with a con artist. You can never win because the conclusion has already been decided from the get go. That's what makes these pseudoskeptics dishonest and not what they claim at all.

But the reality is that for some common paranormal phenomenon such as ESP [extrasensory perception], there is plenty of long standing evidence of both types—anecdotal and scientific. Controlled scientific experiments have yielded positive results for ESP for many years. From the 1930s with JB Rhine, to the current day with Dr. Charles Tart, Dr. Gary Schwartz, Rupert Sheldrake, and many other scientists, positive and consistent results for psi have been found to exist far above chance under controlled conditions. And series of psi experiments that have been replicated for decades known as The Ganzfeld Experiments, Autoganzfeld Experiments and PEAR (Princeton Engineering Anomalies Research) have yielded statistically significant and consistent results above chance as well.

In addition, the anecdotal and experiential evidence is overwhelming. Studies show that at least half the population of the world has had paranormal experiences, and according to the National Science Foundation, *60% of Americans either AGREE or STRONGLY AGREE that some people either possess psychic abilities or extrasensory perception.* That's A LOT, no doubt. Common sense would tell you that if half the people in the world have experienced something, then it's pretty much certain that there's something to it other than fraud, misperception and fantasy, especially since a good number of these experiencers include credible down-to-earth people as well. Likewise, large percentages of people of all types from all walks of life have experienced ghosts too.

Evidence for the Paranormal Is Solid and Robust

So you see, the evidence for such common paranormal phenomena is huge. As parapsychologist author Dean Radin has said, the evidence for psi is so solid and robust that if the same quality of evidence existed for something non-paranormal, it would definitely have been accepted as proven. But because the paranormal is considered taboo in the scientific establishment, there is a sort of censorship and knowledge filtration toward it. There is an automatic negative stigma and bias toward it that assumes that only crackpots believe in such things. So any scientist who openly supports the legitimacy of paranormal phenomena seriously jeopardizes their career and image among their colleagues. Thus, most scientists who believe in some paranormal phenomena will not declare it publicly, but become closet enthusiasts. Mr. Radin discovered this, as many scientists confided in him their secret unofficial interest and belief that some of the paranormal is real.

Even in regard to UFOs there is plenty of evidence for them, albeit not proof. UFO photos and videos are controversial and vague of course, but many credible eyewitnesses, including air force pilots and astronauts, have seen them. They've also been tracked on radar doing aerial maneuvers that man-made aircraft could not do. (And as you know, hallucinations do not appear on radar.) In one famous official incident known as the Washington Merry Go Round Incident of 1952, jet fighters were scrambled to intercept UFOs after they had been tracked on radar. Afterward, to quell public panic, the incident was quickly dismissed though never fully explained. Nevertheless, something significant happened to trigger the alarm and scrambling of fighters, and it wasn't "zero evidence" for sure. But if you think that UFO evidence is strictly confined to obscure sightings, think again. The famous Bentwaters UFO Incident that occurred on an American military base in England in 1980 involving two dozen military witnesses, including Colonel [Charles] Halt, of an up-close UFO sighting, remains an undebunked and compelling case. And after years of extensive investigations and interviews with alien abductees by Budd Hopkins and John Mack, who wrote books on the phenomenon, they concluded that there was more to the abduction experience than mere hallucination or sleep paralysis. In addition, public coalitions such as The Disclosure Project have brought forth a large pool of high ranking government, military and intelligence officials and insiders, over 400 currently, who have confessed to personal knowledge of government involvement with UFOs and ET [extraterrestrial] technology, and the cover ups and secrecy surrounding it. . . .

Pseudoskeptics Are in a State of Perpetual Denial

Nevertheless, pseudoskeptics who claim to only want evidence continue to declare that "there is no evidence" when they get plenty of it from credible sources. Obviously, they are in a state of *perpetual denial and cognitive dissonance.* They deny and filter out anything that doesn't fit into their materialistic reductionistic view of reality, especially anything that has to do with paranormal or conspiracies, no matter what evidence is presented, even if it's documented and scientific. One thing they are they not open to is possibilities. Any possibility that challenges the views of the establishment is simply not possible to them, even if the claims of the establishment itself are not scientific or contradicted by facts. It doesn't even have to be paranormal, it can be ANYTHING that opposes the official version of events, including conspiracies and lies by corrupt government officials or even the existence of shadow governments (which were acknowledged to exist in the '80s with the Iran Contra scandal). Thus, their bias and blind faith in authority as dogma is revealed.

Even if a highly credible source with a long history of accuracy suddenly makes a paranormal claim or a claim against an established view, they automatically dismiss it as bunk before even looking into it. If they do look into it, it will not be to learn the truth about it, but to debunk it. They will even deny evidence from scientific experiments as well. All the while, they tout, "Show me the evidence. Where's the evidence?" Yet when they are shown the evidence, they merely dismiss it or ignore it, acting as though they heard nothing, then go back to repeating that there's no evidence. I've seen them do this for years, in the media, on websites, in forum discussions, and on my own mailing list. It's as though they were deaf and totally belief oriented, seeing only what they want to see.

The problem for pseudoskeptics is that their denial and cognitive dissonance does NOT erase the evidence from reality. It may erase it from their own minds, but it does not the erase the evidence itself. Thus, it can be said that they are deluded and do not face up to reality.

Some examples of pseudoskeptics' denial of evidence and cognitive dissonance:

- If a psychic or medium gets an amazing hit, either something highly unusual and specific that doesn't apply to everyone or a deep dark secret about you that no one knows, which could NOT have been due to cold reading or guessing, then it means nothing to the pseudoskeptics, who will say that it must have been a lucky guess, or due to fraud or your own faulty memory, because no one has psychic abilities.

- If witnesses experience a ghost, they must have been hallucinating, have an active imagination, or lying. Ghosts don't exist, so it must have been something else.

- If people see UFOs, including trained Air Force pilots and astronauts, then they must have misidentified natural phenomenon, because alien ships don't exist, at least not near Earth. And this is so, even if radar picked up objects performing maneuvers impossible for man-made aircraft.

- If psychic abilities are demonstrated under controlled conditions (e.g. PEAR, Ganzfeld, SRI [Spirit Rescue International]), then there must have been flaws in the protocols or lack of controls, because psychic abilities are not possible. Pseudoskeptics then demand repeatability and peer review. But when they get that, they then ask for more repeatability, from skeptical scientists as well. The bar is continually raised until a skeptical scientist finds or imagines any flaw in the experiments and declares them debunked. Only then are they satisfied. Clearly, they only want a particular result (only chance results), not the truth. If it doesn't get debunked, then they accuse the experimenters of improper controls or deceit, as [skeptic James] Randi is infamous for doing.

- They claim that no psi study that shows positive results has ever been published in credible scientific journals. Yet when they are shown citations that they have, they simply become deaf and ignore them. Then they have the nerve to simply repeat their lie again, as if they never even heard you! This is very infuriating and dishonest.
- If a resuscitated patient has an NDE [near-death experience] or OBE [out-of-body experience] where he/she sees details that they could not have known about, then it must have been lucky guesses or unconscious memories, because there is no soul that can leave the body. . . .

Skeptics Are Not Interested in the Evidence

Here is an interesting example of denial of evidence. I found this blog which misrepresented what SCEPCOP [Scientific Committee to Evaluate PseudoSkeptical Criticism of the Paranormal] is about, labeling it "kooky" as well. So when I tried to clear up her misunderstanding, she replied that she just wanted to see evidence, that's all, insinuating that no one so far had been able to give her any evidence for any paranormal or psychic phenomena. She even wrote in her blog, "If SCEPCOP wants to be taken seriously, all they need to do is present some evidence for the paranormal." This requirement was a cinch, so to get her informed, me and other SCEPCOP folks sent her a host of links, resources, books and videos with the evidence she asked for. In response she became overwhelmed and went to the JREF [James Randi Educational Foundation] forum to ask how she can dismiss so much evidence being directed at her, thus demonstrating that her true agenda was not that of an open-minded truth seeker, but of confirmation bias, seeking only that which supported her belief, or disbelief, in anything paranormal, regardless of facts or evidence. That was a bit deceptive of course, but it's typical behavior of pseudoskeptics to *claim one thing and do another*.

Here are her exact words on the JREF forum, revealing her true agenda and mindset:

> Phew I'm glad there's a thread about this here! I have a blog and I made a post about SCEPCOP a while back . . . they recently found it and a bunch of them have started making massive comments on it, so many LINKS!!! They even made a thread about me on their forum, which I was stupid enough to join . . . it's exhausting reading the threads there so I have no desire to go back.
>
> Maybe you guys could help me out with something . . . they've been giving me all of this "evidence" and recommending books etc. but I have no inclination to read it. They've said that I'm not being skeptical because I haven't looked at their stuff and because I won't read the books . . . really it's because it bores me . . . but they say in order to be truly skeptical or whatever I have to look at everything, and I know that's not true, it's ridiculous that they would expect that of me, but how can I respond to this???

She later admitted that she had no interest in examining the evidence after all, and so didn't feel like investing the time in it. So you might be wondering, why did she ask for evidence then if she wasn't interested in it? That makes no sense of course, is illogical and does not compute. But then again, pseudoskeptics are not about logic or making sense, but about faith based disbelief and fanaticism.

The Psychology Behind Skepticism

Afterlife researcher Dr. Victor Zammit, a member of SCEPCOP, explains the psychology behind the pseudoskeptics' *cognitive dissonance*:

1. PSYCHOLOGY: RATIONALIZATION THROUGH
COGNITIVE DISSONANCE
Let's borrow a page from traditional psychology. When a skeptic receives information—say, scientific proof for the afterlife—

which is fundamentally inconsistent with his or her entrenched cherished beliefs, the skeptic tries to rationalize his/her beliefs to reduce and to offset the intense biological, emotional and mental anxiety. The intense anxiety is created by the information that the afterlife exists.

The skeptic's mind tries to resist and reject this new information (even if the information is the absolute truth)—hence the cognitive (the mind) "dissonance"—between the new information—(i.e., the positive evidence for the afterlife) and the skeptic's own personal beliefs that the afterlife cannot exist.

Closed-minded skepticism is extremely difficult to shift because his/her skepticism is "electrically wired" into the skeptic's neurological, psychological, intellectual and emotional belief system. Thus with absolute certainty, this skeptic inexorably loses all sense of empirical equanimity.

Then the skeptic tries to rationalize his/her own personal beliefs and will try to rubbish, denigrate, dismiss and destroy the new information (including scientific proof of some psychic phenomenon) which gives the skeptic a lot of intense anxiety. This skeptic cannot allow his lifelong deeply cherished beliefs against an afterlife to be proved wrong, to be totally incorrect. So this skeptic will use every trick, every bit of energy and every means to try to rationalize i.e., to reduce cognitive dissonance. She will defend her skepticism, and ridicule and viciously attack any positive evidence for the afterlife—which is causing the anxiety to the skeptic. I repeat, all sense of scientific objectivity will be lost.

"The scientists used brain scanning to test whether individuals have knowledge that cannot be explained through normal perceptual processing."

Evidence of Paranormal Phenomena Has Not Been Found

Health and Medicine Week

In the following viewpoint, the authors discuss a study at Harvard University that used neuroimaging to study extrasensory perception (ESP). The researchers argue that if ESP does exist, participants' brains would respond differently to ESP and non-ESP stimuli. The study showed that participants' brains responded identically to the different stimuli. Researchers concluded that the results do not conclusively disprove the existence of ESP and the paranormal, but it is the best evidence to date against the existence of ESP. Health and Medicine Week *is a newsletter published by NewsRx, a media company that produced newsweeklies on various health topics.*

As you read, consider the following questions:

1. Who is Samuel Moulton?

2. What portion of the adults in the United States believe in ESP?

3. What were the two types of stimuli presented to participants in the ESP study discussed in this article?

Psychologists at Harvard University have developed a new method to study extrasensory perception that, they argue, can resolve the century-old debate over its existence. According to the authors, their study not only illustrates a new method for studying such phenomena, but also provides the strongest evidence yet obtained against the existence of extrasensory perception, or ESP.

The research was led by Samuel Moulton, a graduate student in the department of psychology in the Faculty of Arts and Sciences at Harvard University, with Stephen Kosslyn, the John Lindsley Professor of Psychology at Harvard, and was published in the January 2008 issue of the *Journal of Cognitive Neuroscience*. The scientists used brain scanning to test whether individuals have knowledge that cannot be explained through normal perceptual processing.

The ESP Study

"If any ESP processes exist, then participants' brains should respond differently to ESP and non-ESP stimuli," explains Moulton. "Instead, results showed that participants' brains responded identically to ESP and non-ESP stimuli, despite reacting strongly to differences in how emotional the stimuli were and showing subtle, stimulus-related effects."

Nearly half of the adults in the United States believe in the existence of ESP, which includes telepathy (direct knowledge of another person's thoughts), clairvoyance (direct knowledge of remote events), and precognition (direct knowledge of the future). People commonly report unexplained knowledge of a loved one's death or a telephone caller's identity, for example, and attribute this knowledge to paranormal mental processing.

The U.S. government lent credence to such claims when it revealed that it had spent millions of dollars recruiting and training psychic spies during the Cold War. Furthermore, research studies have been reported that appear to support the existence of ESP, including an influential series of experiments analyzed by psychologist Daryl Bem of Cornell University. These studies, however, gave little insight into the mechanisms—normal or paranormal—that produced the anomalous results. Perhaps more telling, others failed to replicate these results.

To develop a better test of ESP, the authors decided to develop a new method, which directly addressed the presumed source of ESP: namely, the brain. They argue that because the brain enables perception and stores information—even events people don't consciously perceive or information they can't consciously remember—it can offer a much more comprehensive test for ESP than self-report or behavior.

"The brain shows a suppressed response to stimuli that a person has seen before, even when those stimuli were presented subliminally, so the person wasn't consciously aware of having seen them; furthermore, it shows an enhanced response to stimuli that a person is expecting," says Moulton. "Because knowledge and expectation bias brain activation, neuroimaging offers us a uniquely powerful test of subtle perceptual or cognitive processes."

ESP and Non-ESP Stimuli and Their Results

To study whether or not ESP exists, Moulton and Kosslyn presented participants with two types of visual stimuli: ESP stimuli and non-ESP stimuli. These two types of stimuli were identical with one exception: ESP stimuli were not only presented visually, but also were presented telepathically, clairvoyantly, and precognitively to participants.

To present stimuli telepathically, the researchers showed the photographs to the participants' identical twin, relative, romantic

The Unsinkable-Rubber-Duck Syndrome

After more than two and a half decades of investigation by skeptical inquirers, we are continually astonished by the fact that no matter how often we criticize paranormal belief claims, they still persist. Indeed, even if they are thoroughly examined and refuted in one age, they seem to re-emerge within the next and people will continue to believe them in spite of evidence to the contrary. This is what I have called the "unsinkable-rubber-duck syndrome." No doubt many are familiar with a carnival shooting gallery, where customers are induced to shoot down moving metal ducks. Here, even if the ducks are successfully knocked down, they pop right back up again.

Paul Kurtz, Skepticism and Humanism: The New Paradigm. *New Brunswick, NJ: Transaction Publishers, 2001.*

partner, or friend, who was seated in another room. To present stimuli clairvoyantly, the researchers displayed the photographs on a distant computer screen. And to present stimuli precognitively, the researchers showed participants the photographs again in the future.

Does this conclusively prove that ESP does not exist? "No," says Moulton. "You cannot affirm the null hypothesis. But at the same time, some null results are stronger than others. This is the best evidence to date against the existence of ESP. Perhaps most important, this study offers scientists a new way to study ESP that avoids the pitfalls of past approaches."

| "*Perhaps the paranormal is absolutely normal, just not yet understood.*"

Evidence Supports the Existence of Ghosts

Tim Weisberg

In the following viewpoint, a newspaper columnist makes the argument that ghosts are real. After early experiences inspired him to pursue paranormal phenomena, the author claims that he has had multiple encounters with spirits and documented their presence at known paranormal hotspots during investigations. Additionally, he explains that physics supports their existence: Energy cannot be created or destroyed, and energy from human bodies that remain behind after death are ghosts. Factors such as high levels of quartz, running water, and strong electromagnetic fields increase paranormal activity, he suggests. Tim Weisberg is a staff writer for the Standard-Times *in New Bedford, Massachusetts.*

As you read, consider the following questions:

1. What evidence does Weisberg offer of encountering ghosts on investigations?
2. What are residual and intelligent haunts, as described by Weisberg?

3. In the author's view, why are paranormal phenomena ignored by mainstream science?

Ghosts are real.

I know as you grew up, you were told otherwise. Heck, so was I. But now I know different.

When we're young, our minds don't have the barriers that "rationality" puts in place later in life. That's why we can believe pretty much everything and, in turn, are receptive to almost anything. But when it comes to ghosts, Mom and Dad tell us there's no such thing—and since at that point in our lives they're the two smartest people in the world, we have no reason to argue.

However, the experiences I've undergone in pursuit of the paranormal would make anyone a believer.

It all started simply enough, with ghostly activity in my aunt's house when I was younger. Shadows on the wall, faucets and electrical devices turning on and off, strange sounds in the night. Of course, they lived next door to a graveyard. And my young cousin had been playing around with a Ouija board. So these must have been the cause of their haunting, right?

Not exactly. All these factors did was help chip away at the mental barrier, and make the family more open to experiencing what was already going on.

My experiences there led me to turn to the library for more information. At the time, all I could find was Time-Life's "Mysteries of the Unknown" series, but it was a good starting point. From there, I discovered the works of paranormalists Dr. Hans Holzer, Brad Steiger, Ed and Lorraine Warren and Rosemary Ellen Guiley. These writers eventually led me to go even deeper, back to the late 19th-century and early 20th-century works of Charles Fort and Harry Price.

In 2006, I was given the chance to take my passion for the paranormal to the airwaves, when my friend Matt Costa and I began "Spooky Southcoast," our weekly radio program delving into the world of the unknown. With the chance to talk directly to

Redefining the Word "Ghost"

I believe that ghosts are made up of energy that is released from the brain after death. I think that this energy is the power of the mind. The brain has senses such as taste, feel, smell, etc., but what gives all these cells the power to control memory, to control responsibilities and make decisions? This is what I believe to be the so-called "soul", spirit, etc. I think the brain naturally accepts an unknown force of nature. This unknown force of nature began at birth and will go on after death by releasing itself when the brain dies. If ghosts do exist, this is it! That's why it is so important for ghost research to be taken to a professional level. The word "ghost" needs to be taken to a better definition besides the soul of a deceased human. I think the correct definition of ghost should be defined as the electrical energy in the human body released after death. I feel that this sort of process would include all other mammals as well. The energy is electromagnetic.

Brian Roesch, Hunting the Dead. *Lincoln, NE: iUniverse, 2001.*

researchers, authors and other movers and shakers in the paranormal field, my belief that ghosts had to exist became all the firmer.

Since then, I've had numerous opportunities to investigate a number of paranormal hot spots, including frequent investigations at the Lizzie Borden Bed & Breakfast in Fall River, considered by many to be one of the world's most haunted places. I've been choked by unseen hands, pushed up against walls and down stairs by non-corporeal assailants. I've been sworn at by voices on tape that weren't heard audibly in the room in which they were recorded. I've heard growls come out of thin air, and had objects fly at me—and that's all just at Lizzie's house.

And my personal experiences often pale in comparison to those reported by colleagues.

Why Ghosts Exist

But if ghosts do exist, why? Without getting bogged down in a discussion of thermodynamics, the Law of Conservation of Energy—a fundamental concept of physics—tells us all we need to know: Energy cannot be created or destroyed, it can only change forms. And what are human beings, but a collection of energy guided by a singular intelligence? When we pass on, when that energy is no longer needed to operate the electrical system of our bodies, where does it go?

My personal belief is that, for the most part, it dissipates into the "ether," absorbed into the universe. But sometimes, it stays behind, retaining the form it held for so long, going through the same motions it had in the past. This is known as a residual—or replay—haunt, because it can't interact and simply plays out over and over. If the electrical impulses are strong enough, the self-awareness can remain behind as well, in what is known as an intelligent haunt. These are the ghosts that can move objects, imprint their voices or images on recorded media and create all the classic features of a haunting.

So what factors make a haunting able to exist at all? There are certain geological factors, such as a high level of quartz in the soil or in the foundation of a building. Quartz records and amplifies energy, which is why we use it in wristwatches and other digital devices. If you investigate an old "haunted" house, chances are you'll find a fieldstone foundation, which is high in quartz.

Other factors like running water and a high electromagnetic field can help the activity ionize and therefore amplify. When paranormal investigators enter a location where a ghost is present, it can actually draw energy directly out of the batteries within their investigation equipment, or even from their own body heat—hence the "cold spots" that develop surrounding ghostly activity.

The Pursuit of the Paranormal Is Science

Make no mistake, the pursuit of the paranormal, when properly conducted, is science. It's just not mainstream science. This has nothing to do with the concepts within the paranormal, but rather with one simple fact: There's no money in proving the supernatural. The days of science for science's sake are long gone. Today, research requires money, and since there's no money to be made off the paranormal, nobody wants to sink any into proving it.

But there are many scientists who do believe, and some are even willing to put their reputations on the line with the more straitlaced scientific community. My good friend and "Spooky Southcoast" co-host Matt Moniz is a chemist by day and paranormal researcher by night. He has done DNA testing on Bigfoot hair samples, testing of UFO landing site soil and other assorted debris, and he's captured quite a bit of convincing evidence when it comes to ghosts.

But he's hardly the first scientist to acknowledge the existence of the paranormal. Albert Einstein certainly felt it was perfectly reasonable under the known laws of physics, and inventor Thomas Edison actually spent the later part of his life working on an electronic device that would allow us to speak directly to the dead. Even Nobel Prize winners like Brian Josephson (physics) and Charles Richet (physiology/medicine) have come forward with their beliefs in the paranormal.

Perhaps the paranormal is absolutely normal, just not yet understood. With reports of activity on the increase and a 2005 Gallup poll showing that 38 percent of Americans believe in ghosts, we're getting closer to accepting and acknowledging that the Great Beyond isn't that far away.

So the next time you hear a howling wind or see the shadow of leaves brushing across your window, it's just that. It's not a ghost.

But that doesn't mean one isn't there.

"Despite the efforts of thousands of real-life ghost hunters over the past decade, the evidence for ghosts has not improved."

Evidence Does Not Currently Support the Existence of Ghosts

Benjamin Radford

In the following viewpoint, a paranormal investigator claims that the existence of ghosts has not been proven by the current body of research. He argues that the types of evidence presented by ghost hunters—from photographed orbs to results from ghost-detecting equipment—are produced by unscientific techniques or have logical explanations. While stating that ghost hunters have a history of total failure in paranormal research, the author does not dismiss the possibilities that ghosts are real, and legitimate evidence can be found. Benjamin Radford is deputy editor of the science magazine Skeptical Inquirer *and a research fellow with the Committee for Skeptical Inquiry.*

As you read, consider the following questions:

1. In reality, what are orbs in photographs, as described by Radford?

2. What is the problem with ghost-hunting gear, as stated by the author?

3. As explained by Radford, what psychological process creates electronic voice phenomena?

The new horror film *Paranormal Activity 3* features another set of amateur ghost hunters trying to document evidence of paranormal activity through the use of home video cameras.

The twitchy, grainy video images of demons and ghosts have scared up hundreds of millions of dollars in box office gold in two previous installments of the low-budget franchise.

It's all good fun for spooky cinematic scares. But what about in the real world?

Between one-third and one-half of Americans believe in ghosts, and that belief motivates many to look for evidence of the paranormal. Researcher Sharon Hill of the Doubtful newsblog counted about 2,000 active amateur ghost hunting groups in the United States. Almost all of them are patterned directly after the hit SyFy TV show "Ghost Hunters," which is now in its eighth season of failing to find good evidence of ghosts.

The Types of Evidence Ghost Hunters Provide

Despite the efforts of thousands of real-life ghost hunters over the past decade, the evidence for ghosts has not improved. Typically, the types of evidence offered for the paranormal fall into a few categories:

1. Personal Experiences. Ghost hunters often report personal feelings and experiences like, "I felt we were being watched," or "I felt like something didn't want us there." They also describe, for example, getting goose bumps upon entering a room or panicking at some unseen presence. There's nothing wrong with personal experiences, but they are not evidence of anything other than that people scare themselves in dark, spooky places.

2. Orbs. Many ghost hunters and books on hauntings claim that ghosts can be photographed, appearing as round or oval white shapes called orbs in the images. Many things can create orbs, including insects, dust and flash reflections. Orbs may seem otherworldly because they appear only in photographs and are usually invisible to the naked eye. To those unaware of the real explanations, they can be spooky, but there is nothing paranormal about them.

3. *Ghost Equipment Results.* Ghost investigators often use unscientific and unproven equipment and techniques in their search for spirits. Some use psychics to try and communicate with ghosts. Others use dowsing rods, which have never been scientifically proven to find anything (including water and restless spirits). Still others, striving for some semblance of science, use high-tech devices such as electromagnetic field detectors and infrared cameras.

These devices are commonly sold as ghost hunting gear, but there is no logical or scientific reason to use this equipment when looking for the paranormal. EMF detectors measure electromagnetic fields, not ghosts; infrared cameras reveal the infrared spectrum, not ghosts. There is no evidence that ghosts have anything to do with electromagnetic fields, infrared images, ions, temperature drops, etc.

4. *Electronic Voice Phenomena.* Most ghost hunters, including the "Ghost Hunters" team, use handheld voice recorders in an attempt to capture a supposed ghost voice, or EVP. Often an investigator will hold the recorder while standing in the middle of a room and addressing the supposed spirit, or while walking around. He will later go back and review the recordings at high volume, listening for any faint murmurs, sounds or noises, which

Electromagnetic Field Readings Are Not Real

There is no reason to believe that ghosts, should they exist, would give off an electromagnetic field reading. Some investigators believe that the soul is composed of an electromagnetic field. If it is, it is nearly impossible to measure. If you take the EMF detector and point it directly at your forehead, you will not get a reading. One can assume that the soul . . . would read whether it was inside of it, or out.

Alison Smith, "The Ins and Outs of Ghost Hunting from a Skeptical Perspective," Arkansas Paranormal and Anomalous Studies Team, http://arpast.org.

may be interpreted as ghost voices. For example, a ghost hunter may ask out-loud, "If there's a spirit here, what's your name?"

Often the investigator will get no answer at all; other times, if the ghost hunters wait long enough they'll hear some random sound that could be interpreted as a faint, mumbled name: "Mary." (Or maybe Terry, Kerry, Larry or Barry—never mind the fact that, as disembodied spirits, ghosts presumably do not have vocal cords, a tongue or a mouth that would allow them to speak.)

The problem is that microphones are very sensitive and may record anything from someone whispering in the next room, to wind blowing, to ordinary random sounds from the environment, or even sounds from the ghost hunters themselves. There's no mystery about what causes EVPs, and it has nothing to do with ghosts. EVPs are created by a well-understood psychological process called apophenia, which causes people to "hear" distinct sounds in random white noise patterns such as the background static in an audio recording (like hearing the doorbell or the telephone while one is in the shower).

In the same way that the human brain allows us to "recognize" random patterns, like faces in clouds, our brains allow us to hear words and phrases in random sounds that aren't really there. In fact, EVPs can be easily heard and induced in laboratory experiments; no ghosts required.

Why the Evidence for Ghosts Is Unimpressive

So why is the evidence for ghosts so unimpressive? One possibility is that ghosts do exist, but that ghost hunters are simply not investigating the right way, using pseudoscience instead of real science and critical thinking. Another possibility is that ghosts and the paranormal do not exist, and that the evidence collected for them is simply the result of hoaxes, honest mistakes, misperceptions and misunderstandings.

In case you're wondering what my expertise is, I have personally investigated—and solved—several hauntings and videos where ghosts were supposedly seen on film. One of my most famous cases involved a mysterious ghostly image captured on a courthouse surveillance camera in Santa Fe, NM, that made national news in 2007. I've also written a book on scientific paranormal investigation.

Of course, the fact that ghost hunters have a spotless track record of complete failure does not mean that ghosts don't exist, or that evidence for paranormal activity might not be found tomorrow, on Halloween, or next year. You don't know if you don't look. Science is open to the possibility of ghosts, the paranormal or anything else—but good evidence is needed. Until then, the only place ghost hunters are guaranteed to find the paranormal is in movie theaters.

> "As the incident unfolded, numerous
> UFOs of various shapes and sizes
> appeared near the bases, according
> to a voice recording of deputy base
> commander, Lt. Col. Charles Halt
> during the event."

Evidence Supports the Existence of UFOs

Lee Speigel

In the following viewpoint, the author discusses a television program that examines the occurrences of UFO sightings. The program claims that there is a UFO phenomenon and many government officials stand behind the existence of UFOs. The article states that it is taboo for government officials to discuss UFOs and that the media often ridicule and destroy the credibility of those who do. Lee Speigel is a writer, reporter and paranormal expert.

As you read, consider the following questions:

1. Who is Leslie Kean?
2. What is the Rendlesham Forest incident?

3. What percent of UFO sightings can eb ascribed to credible witnesses, according to the book discussed in the viewpoint?

• In 1986, a Japan Airlines pilot saw what he described as an unidentified flying object over Alaska closely tailing his 747 [jet]. He made an evasive move. His career was thrown into turmoil, but he never recanted what he claimed he saw.

• In 1987, a Federal Aviation Administration executive said the CIA warned him not to talk about UFOs because the public would panic.

• In 1997, former Arizona governor Fife Symington mocked thousands of people who said they saw mysterious lights over Phoenix, calling out a staffer dressed in a cheesy ET [extraterrestrial alien] costume at a press conference. Ten years later, he apologized for lying to the media and the public.

Television Special Examines UFO Sightings

What these events have in common is that they are unveiled on a new two-hour History Channel special, "Secret Access: UFOs on the Record," that features in-depth accounts from people who have been willing to risk their jobs and reputations to speak out about their remarkable experiences with UFOs.

"The theme of the program is that UFOs exist, but there's a small percentage of sightings that are significant and haven't been explained," said Leslie Kean, author of the *New York Times* bestseller *UFOs: Generals, Pilots and Government Officials Go on the Record*, which forms the basis of the History Channel special.

"There is a phenomenon here and there are many high level officials, including pilots and government people, who have been involved with it and who stand behind the existence of UFOs.

"We make the point that we don't know what they are and that there are a significant number of cases that need to be studied further," Kean told the *Huffington Post*.

The Rendlesham Forest Incident

One compelling case presented in "Secret Access," which has become known as the Rendlesham Forest incident, involved more than 50 military eyewitnesses stationed at the joint U.S. Air Force/NATO bases, Bentwaters and Woodbridge, in Suffolk [England] in 1980.

As the incident unfolded, numerous UFOs of various shapes and sizes appeared near the bases, according to a voice recording of deputy base commander, Lt. Col. Charles Halt during the event.

"This was something of intelligent control beyond any technology we know," Halt told this reporter several months ago. "It's my firm belief that it was extraterrestrial or from a different dimension."

The Phoenix Lights Incident

Then there's the remarkable case involving former Arizona governor Fife Symington, which began on the night of March 13, 1997, when crowds of citizens reported gigantic, silent craft moving around in the skies around Phoenix and which took off silently at blazing speeds. Witnesses included police officers, pilots, military personnel and—as was finally revealed 10 years later—Symington himself.

The two-term governor was at home, watching television when news came on announcing UFO reports in the nearby area. Symington's security detail had gone for the day, and he decided to get into his car alone and check it out.

"I was expecting to see something in the distance, but was awestruck when this thing went overhead. It was moving steadily and quietly," he told the *Huffington Post*.

Symington's description of the huge boomerang-shaped craft matched many others who also reported it that night.

After three months of local media coverage, the Arizona sightings finally hit the national airwaves and were dubbed the "Phoenix Lights." With growing public demand for an explanation, Symington—still tight-lipped about his own sighting—held a national press conference that would haunt him for years.

Claiming to have the culprit responsible for the Phoenix Lights, the governor introduced his chief of staff dressed as an alien and wearing handcuffs. As his staffer was unmasked, Symington told the press, "This just goes to show that you guys are entirely too serious."

Officials Who Discuss UFOs Risk Ridicule

Ten years after his phony alien stunt, Symington finally fessed up about his own dramatic 1997 Phoenix sighting.

"Well, I was confronted by good citizens who were really upset with me, and I didn't realize the depth of their anger. It just really bothered my conscience, so I felt I really needed to square with the truth and that's what I did."

Symington admits there's a taboo about elected officials talking about UFOs.

"I think if you hold a high public office, that the minute you start talking about UFOs or extraterrestrials or anything of that nature, the media immediately tees off and ridicules it. I often refer to the media culture in our country as the culture of ridicule.

"So, everybody reaches for their ridicule gun first before they seriously address the issue when it comes to the matter of UFOs. If you're an elected official, you really need to be careful about what you say, because the media can just totally destroy your credibility."

The Book Behind the Television Special

"Secret Access" isn't the first UFO program presented by the History Channel, according to Julian Hobbs, vice president of development and production.

"Explaining UFOs." © Copyright 2006 by Cameron Cardow, the Ottawa Citizen, and Cagle Cartoons.com.

"History [Channel] doesn't necessarily believe or disbelieve in UFOs. In this case, what really caught our eye about Leslie's book was this idea that 95 percent of all UFO sightings can be pretty easily dismissed—it's the 5 percent in which you have literally governors, military officials, pilots—people normally considered to be level-headed, sane and credible," Hobbs told the *Huffington Post*.

"There wouldn't be the film without the book. When I read Leslie's book, on which the film is based, it changed my opinion about the fact that I think it's worth further investigation into these phenomena," Hobbs added.

Kean, herself, is optimistic about potential contact with extraterrestrials.

"I would hope that they are benign visitors from other planets—that they would be something that could in some way benefit our own struggle on this planet," Kean said. "Even if we knew that we were not alone in the universe, somehow that knowledge alone could affect how we perceive ourselves and maybe affect the future of our civilization."

And Symington is much more outspoken on the subject now than he was while governor of Arizona.

"I know what I saw. To me, there's no question that we've experienced extraterrestrial visits and civilizations that are far more advanced than we are," he suggested.

"I don't approach it from a fearful standpoint. I actually like to think that we're not alone in the universe, and I'm not bashful on the subject. I think we're dealing with some fascinating unknowns and someday, the truth will out."

> "If investigators are unable to find the explanation for a particular UFO case, that doesn't constitute proof that the case is unexplainable."

Evidence Does Not Support the Existence of UFOs

James Oberg

In the following viewpoint, a space analyst writes that evidence of UFOs is insufficient, and recent testimony from military and commercial pilots is not credible. Rather than being infallible observers of the sky, the author contends, pilots are more likely to interpret objects and atmospheric phenomena—from weather balloons to meteors—on hazardous terms, demonstrating a bias in what they witness. In conclusion, he opposes assumptions that unusual and unexplained aerial sightings are automatically paranormal. James Oberg is a space analyst for NBC News, veteran of NASA Mission Control, and author of several books on space exploration and policies.

As you read, consider the following questions:

1. In comparison to the best class of witnesses, what figures does Oberg cite for the misperception rates of military and commercial pilots?

2. As described in the viewpoint, what does Ronald Fisher emphasize in interviewing eyewitnesses?

3. How does Oberg respond to evidence that UFOs are guided by intelligent pilots?

If we trust pilots to carry us through the air safely, and to guard our nation's skies, then why can't we trust what they tell us about their encounters with unidentified flying objects?

That's the question posed by investigative journalist Leslie Kean in her new book, *UFOs: Generals, Pilots and Government Officials Go on the Record*. It's a compelling question—but is it a good argument for the existence of something truly unexplainable?

The book's main themes are the extraordinary stories of strange aerial encounters in Europe, South America and even the United States. In these stories, investigators have failed to pinpoint phenomena to explain the sightings. And because the primary witnesses are pilots, the accounts are considered more credible than run-of-the-mill UFO reports. But are they really?

Kean asserts that pilots are the best describers of aerial phenomena. "They represent the world's best-trained observers of everything that flies," she writes. "What better source for data on UFOs is there? . . . [They] are among the least likely of any group of witnesses to fabricate or exaggerate reports of strange sightings."

This may sound like a plausible assumption, but others who have studied the raw evidence disagree. Experienced UFO investigators realize that pilots, who instinctively and quite properly interpret visual phenomena in the most hazardous terms, are not dispassionate observers. For pilots, a split-second diagnosis can be a matter of life or death—and so they're inclined to overestimate the potential threats posed by what they see.

One of the world's first genuine UFO investigators, Allen Hynek of Northwestern University, came to believe that some encounters really could have otherworldly causes. But he was much more skeptical about the reliability of pilot testimony. "Surprisingly, commercial and military pilots appear to make relatively poor witnesses," he wrote in "The Hynek UFO Report."

Hynek found that the best class of witnesses had a 50 percent misperception rate, but that pilots had a much higher rate: 88 percent for military pilots, 89 percent for commercial pilots, the worst of all categories listed. Pilots could be counted on for an accurate identification of familiar objects—such as aircraft and ground structures—but Hynek said "it should come as no surprise that the majority of pilot misidentifications were of astronomical objects."

The authors of a Russian UFO study came to the same conclusion. Yuli Platov of the Soviet Academy of Science and Col. Boris Sokolov of the Ministry of Defense looked into a series of sightings in 1982 that caused air defense units to scramble jet fighters to intercept the UFOs. Platov and Sokolov said the sightings were sparked by military balloons that rose to higher-than-expected altitudes.

"The described episodes show that even experienced pilots are not immune against errors in the evaluation of the size of observed objects, the distances to them, and their identification with particular phenomena," Platov wrote.

Pilots Are Susceptible to Overinterpretation

Ronald Fisher of the International Forensic Research Institute at Florida International University in Miami is a lecturer who teaches staff members at the National Transportation Safety Board how to interview eyewitnesses at "critical events" such as airplane crashes. He stresses the importance of eliciting raw sensory impressions first, before asking for the witness's interpretation of what they think they saw.

"Once they start focusing on their interpretation, that will color the memory of their perceptions," he told Msnbc.com.

"Pilots are susceptible to overinterpretation, especially of vague, rapid and unclear experiences," he continued. "The less clear the situation, the more your general knowledge and your expectations [contribute]." Passage of time is an enemy of accuracy, because it gives witnesses the opportunity "to use their general knowledge to construct the memory of what they experienced."

As witnesses of things seen while flying, pilots were a special case, "The cost of a false negative is greater than the cost of a false positive," he explained. "It's probably a safety mechanism."

The body of UFO reports is replete with cases of spectacular misinterpretations, and pilots are frequently involved. So it's prudent to use caution when evaluating the testimony of pilots.

Pilots Have "Observer Bias"

UFOs are often reported as maneuvering intelligently, and Kean argues that a particularity of the different types of maneuvers reported by pilots serves as proof that UFOs are real and are acting with intelligence. But that logic actually ends up supporting the idea that a pilot's circumstances affect what he or she reports seeing.

Kean refers to the "Weinstein List," a compendium of 1,300 UFO reports from pilots, assembled by French investigator Dominique Weinstein in 2001. It is described as containing only those "cases for which adequate data is available to categorize the [cause] as unknowns."

"One crucial point I have noted, which is shown in Weinstein's study, is that a UFO's behavior tends to depend on whether the encounter involves a military aircraft or a civilian passenger plane," Kean writes.

"Neutrality usually seems the general rule with commercial airlines or private planes, whereas an active interaction often occurs between UFOs and military aircraft. Military pilots usually described the movements of UFOs as they would air maneuvers of conventional aircraft, using terms such as follows,

A Stable UFO Intellectual Community Does Not Exist

The "great UFO books" that you will read contain materials probably thrice-distorted. But doesn't that happen in all fields of academic study, and we seem to survive? Perhaps. But in academia there is some form of truly interacting, critiquing, and challenging community. It doesn't work very efficiently, but in some fields at least it seems to ultimately sift wheat from chaff. There has been no such stable UFO intellectual community. There are few proper fora, and until recently there were none at all. There are arguments a plenty, but they occur independently of any proper mode of lasting evaluation.

Michael D. Swords, "A Guide to UFO Research," Journal of Scientific Exploration, *vol. 7, no. 1, 1993.*

flees, acute turns, in formation, close collision, and aerial combat," she says.

For Kean, this constitutes evidence that the UFOs are guided by intelligent pilots. "These incidents clearly demonstrate that in no way are these examples of natural events, but rather that UFOs are phenomena with a deliberate behavior. The physical nature of UFOs has been proved," she says.

But a much simpler explanation makes more sense: The difference is due to "observer bias." People see what they expect to see, and combat pilots expect to encounter combative bogies. Civilian pilots mostly fear accidental collisions.

The different behavior that is *perceived* by the two categories of pilots doesn't necessarily mean the unidentified flying objects themselves behave differently. It's more likely that different kinds of pilots draw upon differently developed instincts as they react to perceived threats—and thus they bring different interpretations to stimuli that are actually similar.

UFO Claims Must Be Examined Critically

There's no reason to argue that all the pilot reports are caused by exactly the same stimuli. UFO reports that are linked to rocket launches or booster re-entries are relatively easy to explain, because the location and timing of the events can be correlated with the accounts from startled and mistaken witnesses.

For other stimuli, such as fireball meteors, secret (or illegal) aircraft operations or natural atmospheric displays, documentation of their transitory existence usually doesn't exist. The main value of the solved UFO cases is to allow a definitive calibration of pilot testimony in general.

Thus, I am not dismayed by the fact that I can't explain every case Kean mentions in her book, because experience has shown that finding the real explanation—even if it turns out to be prosaic—is often a massive effort involving as much luck as sweat. If investigators are unable to find the explanation for a particular UFO case, that doesn't constitute proof that the case is unexplainable.

This is just a fact of life, for UFO sleuths as well as other breeds of investigators. The same is true for murders, kidnappings, accidents, illnesses—for all the catastrophes that befall humanity. We don't need to conjure up alien murderers or kidnappers to account for unsolved crimes. Not finding [labor union leader] Jimmy Hoffa isn't proof he must be on Mars.

So the "not proven" assessment makes it even *more* important to keep our eyes and minds open—to vigorously observe, accurately perceive, and precisely relate unusual aerial perceptions. Something really new could still be discovered. Or something critically important could be masquerading, by accident or design, in a manner that leads too many people to pay too little attention.

Accepting every UFO claim uncritically or rejecting every claim automatically would be equally unjustified. And quite possibly, equally harmful.

> *"Our brain has the ability to not only reflect on past experiences, but also anticipate future experiences."*

Evidence Supports the Existence of Psychic Phenomena

Melissa Burkley

In the following viewpoint, a psychology professor asserts that cutting-edge research supports psychic phenomena. In one study cited by the author, the ability to "reach back in time" to perform recall was demonstrated. Another study indicated that the brain has the ability to know what is coming next and make a decision. While this research has limitations, she notes, it shows that some individuals are more attuned to psychic capability. Melissa Burkley is an assistant professor of social psychology at Oklahoma State University.

As you read, consider the following questions:

1. According to Burkley, what effects did Daryl Bern use in his studies?

2. What type of people in the studies demonstrates stronger effects, as told by Burkley?

3. What has quantum physics shown about behavior and future events, as claimed by Burkley?

In Lewis Carroll's *Through the Looking Glass*, the White Queen tells Alice that in her land, "memory works both ways." Not only can the Queen remember things from the past, but she also remembers "things that happened the week after next." Alice attempts to argue with the Queen, stating "I'm sure mine only works one way . . . I can't remember things before they happen." The Queen replies, "It's a poor sort of memory that only works backwards."

How much better would our lives be if we could live in the White Queen's kingdom, where our memory would work backwards and forwards? For instance, in such a world, you could take an exam and then study for it afterwards to make sure you performed well in the past. Well, the good news is that according to a recent series of scientific studies by Daryl Bem, you already live in that world!

Dr. Bem, a social psychologist at Cornell University, conducted a series of studies that will soon be published in one of the most prestigious psychology journals (*Journal of Personality and Social Psychology*). Across nine experiments, Bem examined the idea that our brain has the ability to not only reflect on past experiences, but also anticipate future experiences. This ability for the brain to "see into the future" is often referred to as psi phenomena.

The Studies Rely on Standard Scientific Methods

Although prior research has been conducted on the psi phenomena—we have all seen those movie images of people staring at Zener cards with a star or wavy lines on them—such studies often fail to meet the threshold of "scientific investigation." However, Bem's studies are unique in that they represent standard scientific methods and rely on well-established principles in psychology. Essentially, he took effects that are considered valid and reliable in psychology—studying improves memory, priming facilitates response times—and simply reversed their chronological order.

For example, we all know that rehearsing a set of words makes them easier to recall in the future, but what if the rehearsal occurs after the recall? In one of the studies, college students were given a list of words and after reading the list, were given a surprise recall test to see how many words they remembered. Next, a computer randomly selected some of the words on the list as practice words and the participants were asked to retype them several times. The results of the study showed that the students were better at recalling the words on the surprise recall test that they were later given, at random, to practice. According to Bem, practicing the words after the test somehow allowed the participants to "reach back in time to facilitate recall."

In another study, Bem examined whether the well-known priming effect could also be reversed. In a typical priming study, people are shown a photo and they have to quickly indicate if the photo represents a negative or positive image. If the photo is of a cuddly kitten, you press the "positive" button and if the photo is of maggots on rotting meat, you press the "negative" button. A wealth of research has examined how subliminal priming can speed up your ability to categorize these photos. Subliminal priming occurs when a word is flashed on the computer screen so quickly that your conscious brain doesn't recognize what you saw, but your nonconscious brain does. So you just see a flash, and if I asked you to tell me what you saw, you wouldn't be able to. But deep down, your nonconscious brain saw the word and processed it. In priming studies, we consistently find that people who are primed with a word consistent with the valence of the photo will categorize it quicker. So if I quickly flash the word "happy" before the kitten picture, you will click the "positive" button even quicker, but if I instead flash the word "ugly" before it, you will take longer to respond. This is because priming you with the word "happy" gets your mind ready to see happy things.

In Bem's retroactive priming study, he simply reversed the time sequence on this effect by flashing the primed word *after* the person categorized the photo. So I show you the kitten picture, you pick whether it is positive or negative, and then I randomly choose to prime you with a good or bad word. The results showed that people were quicker at categorizing photos when it was followed by a consistent prime. So not only will you categorize the kitten quicker when it is preceded by a good word, you will also categorize it quicker when it is followed by a good word. It was as if, while participants were categorizing the photo, their brain knew what word was coming next and this facilitated their decision.

These are just two examples of the studies that Bem conducted, but his other studies showed similar "retroactive" effects. The results clearly suggest that average "non-psychic" people seem to be able to anticipate future events.

The Studies Are Small but Highly Consistent

One question you may be asking is how big of a difference was there? Does studying for a test after it has occurred, or priming you with a word after categorizing the photo make a dramatic change, or is it just a slight bump in performance? Essentially, these are questions of "effect size." It is true that the effect sizes in Bem's studies are small (e.g., only slightly larger than chance). However, there are several reasons why we shouldn't just disregard these results based on small, but highly consistent, effect sizes.

First, across his studies, Bem did find that certain people demonstrate stronger effects than others. In particular, people high in stimulus seeking—an aspect of extraversion where people respond more favorably to novel stimuli—showed effect sizes nearly twice the size of the average person. This suggests that some people are more sensitive to psi effects than others.

Parapsychology Enriches Behavioral Science

In the final analysis what fairly can be said of parapsychology? . . . [As] far as spontaneous cases are concerned it seems likely that there are numerous instances of self-deception, delusion, and even fraud. Some of the empirical literature likewise might be attributable to shoddy experimental procedures and to fraudulent manipulation of data. Be that as it may, there is sound phenomenological evidence of parapsychological experiences and experimental evidence of anomalous events too, and to this extent behavioral scientists ethically are obliged to encourage the investigation of these phenomena rather than dismissing them out of hand. If all of the phenomena do prove to be explicable within conventional principles of mainstream psychology surely that is something worth knowing . . . and if just one of the phenomena should be found to demand a revision or an expansion of contemporary psychological principles, how enriched behavioral science would be.

Harvey J. Irwin and Caroline A. Watt, An Introduction to Parapsychology. *Jefferson, NC: McFarland & Co., 2007.*

Second, small effect sizes are not that uncommon in psychology (and other sciences). For example, on average, the Bem studies showed an effect size of .20 (out of a possible range of 0–1). Although that is fairly small, it is as large as or larger than some well-established effects, including the link between aspirin and heart attack prevention, calcium intake and bone mass, second hand smoke and lung cancer, and condom use and HIV prevention. And as [statistician Jacob] Cohen has pointed out, such small effect sizes are most likely to occur in the early stages of exploring a topic, when scientists are just starting to discover why the effect occurs and when it is most likely to occur.

Psi Phenomena Relate to Modern Science

So if we accept that these psi phenomena are real, how then can we explain them without throwing out our entire understanding of time and physics? Well, the truth is that these effects are actually pretty consistent with modern physics' take on time and space. For example, Einstein believed that the mere act of observing something here could affect something there, a phenomenon he called "spooky action at a distance."

Similarly, modern quantum physics has demonstrated that light particles seem to know what lies ahead of them and will adjust their behavior accordingly, even though the future event hasn't occurred yet. For example, in the classic "double slit experiment," physicists discovered that light particles respond differently when they are observed. But in 1999, researchers pushed this experiment to the limits by asking "what if the observation occurred after the light particles were deployed." Surprisingly, they found the particles acted the same way, as if they knew they were going to be observed in the future even though it hadn't happened yet.

Such trippy time effects seem to contradict common sense and trying to make sense of them may give the average person a headache, but physicists have just had to accept it. As Dr. [Raymond] Chiao, a physicist from Berkeley once said about quantum mechanics, "It's completely counterintuitive and outside our everyday experience, but we (physicists) have kind of gotten used to it."

So although humans perceive time as linear, it doesn't necessarily mean it is so. And as good scientists, we shouldn't let our preconceived beliefs and biases influence what we study, even if these preconceived beliefs reflect our basic assumptions about how time and space work.

Dr. Bem's work is thought provoking, and like good cutting-edge science is supposed to do, it offers more questions than answers. If we suspend our beliefs about time and accept that the brain is capable of reaching into the future, the next question becomes "how does it do this?" Just because the effect seems "supernatural" doesn't necessarily mean the cause is. Many scientific discoveries were once considered outlandish and more suited to science fiction (e.g., the earth being round, microscopic organisms). Future research is greatly needed to explore the exact reasons for these studies' effects.

Like many novel explorations in science, Bem's findings may have a profound effect on what we know and have come to accept as true. But for some of you, perhaps these effects are not such a big surprise, because somewhere deep down inside, you already knew you would be reading about them today!

"Whenever they have data that, by some statistical formula, is not likely due to chance, they attribute the outcome to psi."

Evidence Does Not Support the Existence of Psychic Phenomena

Robert Todd Carroll

In the following viewpoint, a philosopher refutes research that supports psychic abilities. Focusing on parapsychologist Dean Radin, he argues that Radin's analyses demonstrate very weak statistical evidence for the presence of psi phenomena. He adds that Radin offers implausible speculations on the benefits of mind over matter in technology, research, and society. Consequently, the author dismisses parapsychology as a legitimate area of science. Robert Todd Carroll is a former philosophy professor at Sacramento City College and author of the Skeptic's Dictionary, *a book of material compiled from his website of the same name.*

As you read, consider the following questions:

1. What do believers in psi use as evidence for their beliefs, according to the author?

2. What makes a well-designed study in parapsychology, in Carroll's words?

3. What is the best argument for psi phenomena that Radin can come up with, as said by Carroll?

Dean Radin, author of *The Conscious Universe: The Scientific Truth of Psychic Phenomena*, says that "psi [parapsychology] researchers have resolved a century of skeptical doubts through thousands of replicated laboratory studies" regarding the reality of psychic phenomena such as ESP (extrasensory perception) and PK (psychokinesis). Of course, Radin also considers meta-analysis as the most widely accepted method of measuring *replication*. Few scientists would agree with either of these claims. In any case, most American adults—about 75%, according to a 2005 Gallup poll—believe in at least one paranormal phenomenon. Forty-one percent believe in ESP. Fifty-five percent believe in the power of the mind to heal the body. One doesn't need to be psychic to know that the majority of believers in psi have come to their beliefs through experience or anecdotes, rather than through studying the scientific evidence Radin puts forth in his book.

Radin doesn't claim that the scientific evidence is going to make more believers. He realizes that the kind of evidence psi researchers have put forth hasn't persuaded most scientists that there is anything of value in parapsychology. He thinks there is "a general uneasiness about parapsychology" and that because of the "insular nature of scientific disciplines, the vast majority of psi experiments are unknown to most scientists." He also dismisses critics as skeptics who've conducted "superficial reviews." Anyone familiar with the entire body of research, he says, would recognize he is correct and would see that there are "fantastic theoretical implications" to psi research. Nevertheless, in 2005 the Nobel Committee once again passed over the psi scientists when handing out awards to those who have made significant contributions to our scientific knowledge.

Radin Offers a Hodgepodge of Occult Statistics

The evidence Radin presents, however, is little more than a hodgepodge of occult statistics. Unable to find a single person who can correctly guess a three-letter word or move a pencil an inch without trickery, the psi researchers have resorted to doing complex statistical analyses of data. In well-designed studies they assume that whenever they have data that, by some statistical formula, is not likely due to chance, they attribute the outcome to psi. A well-designed study is one that carefully controls for such things as cheating, sensory leakage (unintentional transfer of information by non-psychic means), inadequate randomization, and other factors that might lead to an artifact (something that looks like it's due to psi when it's actually due to something else).

The result of this enormous data that Radin cites is that there is statistical evidence (for what it's worth) that indicates (however tentatively) that some very weak psi effects are present (so weak that not a single individual who participates in a successful study has any inkling of possessing psychic power). Nevertheless, Radin thinks it is appropriate to speculate about the enormous implications of psi for biology, psychology, sociology, philosophy, religion, medicine, technology, warfare, police work, business, and politics. Never mind that nobody has any idea as to how psi might work. That is a minor detail to someone who can write with a straight face (apparently) that:

> Lots of independent, simple glimpses of the future may one day innocently crash the future. It's not clear what it means to "crash the future," but it doesn't sound good.

No, it certainly doesn't sound good. But, as somebody once said, "the future will be better tomorrow."

A Return to Magical Thinking

According to Radin, we may look forward to a future with "psychic garage-door openers" and the ability to "push atoms around" with our minds. Radin is not the least bit put off by the criticism that all the other sciences have led us away from superstition and magical thinking, while parapsychology tries to lead us into those pre-scientific modes. Radin notes that "the concept that mind is primary over matter is deeply rooted in Eastern philosophy and ancient beliefs about magic." However, instead of saying that it is now time to move forward, he rebuffs "Western science" for rejecting such beliefs as "mere superstition." Magical thinking, he says, "lies close beneath the veneer of the sophisticated modern mind." He even claims that "the fundamental issues [of consciousness] remain as mysterious today as they did five thousand years ago." We may not have arrived at a final theory of the mind, but a lot of the mystery has evaporated with the progress made in the neurosciences over the past century. None of our advancing knowledge of the mind, however, has been due to contributions from parapsychologists.

Radin doesn't grasp the fact that the concept of mind can be an illusion without being a "meaningless illusion." He seems to have read [philosopher] David Chalmers, but I suggest he and his followers read [philosopher and cognitive scientist] Daniel Dennett. I'd begin with *Sweet Dreams*. Consciousness is not "a complete mystery," as Radin claims. The best that Radin can come up with as evidence that psi research has something to offer consciousness studies is the claim that "information can be obtained in ways that bypass the ordinary sensory system altogether." Let's ignore the fact that this claim begs the question. What neuroscience has uncovered is just how interesting and complex this "ordinary sensory system" turns out to be.

Magical Thinking Is Essential

Radin would have us believe that magical thinking is essential to our psychological well being. If he's right, we'll one day be able to solve all social problems by "mass-mind healings." And religious claims will get new meaning as people come to understand the psychic forces behind miracles and talking to the dead. According to Radin, when a medium today talks to a spirit "perhaps he is in contact with someone who is alive in the *past*. From the 'departed' person's perspective, she may find herself communicating with someone from the future, although it is not clear that she would know that." Yes, I don't think that would be clear, either.

In medicine, Radin expects distant mental healing (which he argues has been scientifically established) to expand to something that "might be called techno-shamanism." He describes this new development as "an exotic, yet rigorously schooled combination of ancient magical principles and future technologies." He expects psi to join magnetic resonance imaging and blood tests as common stock in the world of medicine. "This would translate into huge savings and improved quality of life for millions of people" as "untold billions of dollars in medical costs could be saved."

Then, of course, there will be the very useful developments that include the ability to telepathically "call a friend in a distant spacecraft, or someone in a deeply submerged submarine." On the other hand, the use of psychic power by the military and by police investigators will depend, Radin says, on "the mood of the times." If what is popular on television is an indicator of the mood of the times, I predict that there will be full employment for psychic detectives and remote viewers in the future.

Radin looks forward to the day when psi technology "might allow thought control of prosthetics for paraplegics" and "mind-melding techniques to provide people with vast, computer-enhanced memories, lightning-fast mathematical capabilities, and supersensitive perceptions." He even suggests we employ remote viewer Joe McMoneagle to reveal future technological devices he "has sensed in his remote-viewing sessions."

Radin considers a few other benefits that will come from our increased ability to use psi powers: "to guide archeological digs and treasure-hunting expeditions, enhance gambling profits, and provide insight into historical events." However, he does not consider some of the obvious problems and benefits that would occur should psychic ability become common. Imagine the difficulties for the junior high teacher in a room full of adolescents trained in PK. Teachers and parents would be spending most of their psychic energy controlling the hormones of their charges. The female garment and beauty industries would be destroyed as many attractive females would be driven to try to make themselves look ugly to avoid having their clothes being constantly removed by psychic perverts and pranksters.

[Paranormal investigator and skeptic] Ben Radford has noted the potential for "gross and unethical violations of privacy," as people would be peeping into each other's minds. On the other hand, infidelity and all forms of deception might die out, since nobody could deceive anyone about anything if we were all psychic. Magic would become pointless and "professions that involve deception would be worthless." There wouldn't be any need for undercover work or spies. Every child molester would be identified immediately. No double agent could ever get away with it. There wouldn't be any more lotteries, since everybody could predict the winning numbers. We wouldn't need trials of accused persons and the polygraph would be a thing of the past. . . .

Radin notes only one problem should psi ability become common: we'll all be dipping into the future and we might "crash the future," whatever that means. The bright side of crashing the future will be the realization of "true freedom" as we will no longer be doomed to our predestined fate. We will all have the power "to create the future as we wish, rather than blindly follow a predetermined course through our ignorance." That should make even the most cynical Islamic fundamentalist or doomsday Christian take heed. This psi stuff could be dangerous to one's delusions even as it tickles one's funny bone and stimulates one's imagination to aspire to the power of gods and demons.

Explaining Everything but Illuminating Nothing

Radin has a follow-up book out called *Entangled Minds: Extrasensory Experiences in a Quantum Reality*. Like *The Conscious*

Universe, this one lays out the scientific evidence for psi as seen from the eyes of a true believer. As noted above, in *The Conscious Universe*, Radin uses statistics and meta-analysis to prove that psychic phenomena really do exist even if those who have the experiences in the labs are unaware of them. Statistical data show that the world has gone psychic, according to the latest generation of parapsychologists. You may be unconscious of it, but your mind is affecting random number generators all over the world as you read this. The old psychic stuff—thinking about aunt Hildie moments before she calls to tell you to bugger off—is now demonstrated to be true by statistical methods that were validated in 1937 by Burton Camp and meta-validated by Radin 60 years later when he asserted that meta-analysis was the replication parapsychologists had been looking for. The only difference is that now when you think of aunt Hildie it might be moments before she calls her car mechanic and that, too, may be linked to activity in your mind that you are un-aware of.

Radin's second book sees *entanglement* as a key to under-standing extrasensory phenomena. Entanglement is a concept from quantum physics that refers to connections between sub-atomic particles that persist regardless of being separated by various distances. He notes that some physicists have speculated that the entire universe might be entangled and that the Eastern mystics of old might have been on to something cosmic. His speculations are rather wild but his assertions are rather mod-est. For example: "I believe that entanglement suggests a scenario that may ultimately lead to a vastly improved understanding of psi" and "I propose that the fabric of reality is comprised [sic] of 'entangled threads' that are consistent with the core of psi experi-ence." Skeptics might suggest that studying self-deception and wishful thinking would lead to a vastly improved understand-ing of psi research and that being consistent with a model is a minimal, necessary condition for taking any model seriously, but hardly sufficient to warrant much faith. . . .

Radin predicts that someday "psi research will be taught in universities with the same aplomb as today's elementary economics and biology." Perhaps psi research will be taught in the same classroom as intelligent design, though this seems unlikely as parapsychology attempts to reduce all supernatural and paranormal phenomena to physics. Maybe they could both be taught in the same curriculum: *things that explain everything but illuminate nothing.*

Periodical and Internet Sources Bibliography

The following articles have been selected to supplement the diverse views presented in this chapter.

Brian Abshire	"The Bible and Ghosts," christian-civilization.org, October 31, 2009.
James E. Alcock	"Back from the Future: Parapsychology and the Bem Affair," *Skeptical Inquirer*, March–April 2011.
Tim Brosnan	"Commercial Airline Pilot Says UFOs Are Real," *Technorati*, July 30, 2010.
Martin J. Clemens	"Electronic Voice Phenomenon Is Not Evidence of Ghosts," *Commercial Indignation*, January 12, 2010.
Brian Dunning	"The Scole Experiment," *Skeptoid*, November 10, 2009.
John M. Glionna	"A UFO Cold Case," *Los Angeles Times*, March 18, 2008.
Gary Jensen	"A Rationalist's Ghost Story," *Religious Dispatches*, October 26, 2010.
Jack Mendoza	"The Creepy Scientific Explanation Behind Ghost Sightings," Cracked.com, October 26, 2010.
Kevin Nelson, interviewed by Katherine Don	"'Spiritual Doorway in the Brain': The Science of Near-Death Experiences," *Slate*, January 12, 2011.
Stephanie Pappas	"Controversial Psychic Ability Claim Doesn't Hold up in New Experiments," *LiveScience*, March 14, 2012.
Phil Patton	"Something in the Sky," *Popular Mechanics*, March 2009.
Benjamin Radford	"Do Einstein's Laws Prove Ghosts Exist?," *Life's Little Mysteries*, November 9, 2011.

OPPOSING
VIEWPOINTS®
SERIES

Chapter 2

Why Do People Believe in Paranormal Phenomena?

Chapter Preface

Most researchers and experts are hesitant to draw a conclusive link between mental illness and paranormal beliefs. "Few scholars would seriously embrace this extreme characterization," states Jonathan C. Smith, a psychology professor at Roosevelt University in Chicago, Illinois. But Smith speculates both have similarities that should not be ignored. "There is a type of 'crazy thinking' that is worth exploring," he asserts.

According to Smith, experiences such as communicating with the dead and being abducted by aliens resemble episodes of schizophrenia, a disorder marked by auditory hallucinations and delusional thoughts. "One popular theory is that terrified and confused schizophrenics try to make some sense out of a frightening world by concluding that the voices come from an outside source, like space aliens," he suggests. When faced with a realistic explanation or lack of evidence, he continues, a person with a paranormal mindset justifies or clings onto it to create a form of relief. "I propose that perfectly sane, intelligent, and honest true believers in the paranormal—those who refuse to question or use sensible tools of critical thinking—possess a similar thinking process," Smith contends. For instance, someone who thinks that he experienced an alien abduction will deny any rational causes—such as having a nightmare or sleep paralysis—and expand upon his delusions. "Both a paranormal believer and a schizophrenic can create belief systems of exquisite complexity," he asserts, "rivaling ancient charts of astrology and acupuncture."

Nonetheless, some members of the paranormal community argue that believing in the paranormal can be misinterpreted as a psychological disorder. "Could it be that some people who are diagnosed with some form of a mental illness—whether depression, bipolar disorder, or something else—are actually just more sensitive to the psychic energies of those around them?" asks Karen Frazier, managing editor of *Paranormal Underground*, an online magazine. Frazier claims that the individual could actually have emerging abilities as a psychic or medium, but does not yet understand them. "Maybe, in some cases, it is a highly intuitive, empathic, or sensitive person who hasn't learned to shield themselves from all of the energies that bombard them," she maintains. In the following chapter, authors offer a range of perspectives—from scientific to religious—to explain why people believe in paranormal phenomena.

> *"The emerging consensus is that belief in the supernatural seems to arise from the same mental processes that underlie everyday reasoning and perception."*

Brain Activity Influences Belief in Paranormal Phenomena

Sharon Begley

In the following viewpoint, a science writer states that beliefs in paranormal phenomena result from extremes in normal brain functions. She insists that when mental processes such as perception and reasoning are intensified, such beliefs can form. For instance, the brain fills the gaps in vision and hearing to complete the picture, the author maintains, potentially leading to supernatural misinterpretations of ordinary stimuli. Seeing patterns in coincidences indicates a psychological bias to validate beliefs, she says, and humans developed a high sensitivity to the presence of living beings, creating a tendency to perceive inanimate objects as ghosts. Sharon Begley is the senior health and science correspondent at Reuters, *and a former science editor and columnist at* Newsweek.

As you read, consider the following questions:

1. How does a structure in the superior parietal lobe create a paranormal experience, as explained by Begley?

2. What does brain imaging demonstrate about seeing and hearing imagined things, according to the author?

3. What explanation does the author provide for skepticism if the brain is wired to believe in the paranormal?

It wasn't immediately obvious to Walter Semkiw that he was the reincarnation of John Adams. Adams was a lawyer and rabble-rouser who helped overthrow a government; Semkiw is a doctor who has never so much as challenged a parking ticket. The second president was balding and wore a powdered wig; Semkiw has a full head of hair. But in 1984, a psychic told the then medical resident and psychiatrist-in-training that he is the reincarnation of a major figure of the Revolution, possibly Adams. Once Semkiw got over his skepticism—as a student of the human mind, he was of course familiar with "how people get misled and believe something that might not be true," he recalls—he wasn't going to let superficial dissimilarities dissuade him so easily. As he researched Adams's life, Semkiw began finding many tantalizing details. For instance, Adams described his handwriting as "tight-fisted and concise"—"just like mine," Semkiw realized. He also saw an echo of himself in Adams's dedication to the cause of independence from England. "I can be very passionate," Semkiw says. The details accumulated and, after much deliberation, Semkiw went with his scientific side, dismissing the reincarnation idea.

But one day in 1995, when Semkiw was the medical director for Unocal 76, the oil company, he heard a voice in his head intoning, "Study the life of Adams!" Now he found details much more telling than those silly coincidences he had learned a dozen years earlier. He looked quite a bit like the second president, Semkiw realized. Adams's description of parishioners in church pews as resembling rows of cabbages was "something I would have said," Semkiw realized. "We are both very visual." And surely it was telling that Unocal's slogan was "the spirit of '76."

It was all so persuasive, thought Semkiw, who is now a doctor at the Kaiser Permanente Medical Group in California, that as a man of science and reason whose work requires him to critically evaluate empirical evidence, he had to accept that he was Adams reincarnated.

Perhaps you don't believe that Semkiw is the reincarnation of John Adams. Or that playwright August Wilson is the reincarnation of Shakespeare, or George W. Bush the reincarnation of Daniel Morgan, a colonel in the American Revolution who was known for his "awkward speech" and "coarse manners," as Semkiw chronicles on his Web site johnadams.net. But if you don't believe in reincarnation, then the odds are that you have at least felt a ghostly presence behind you in an "empty" house. Or that you have heard loved ones speak to you after they passed away. Or that you have a lucky shirt. Or that you can tell when a certain person is about to text you, or when someone unseen is looking at you. For if you have never had a paranormal experience such as these, and believe in none of the things that science says do not exist except as tricks played on the gullible or—as neuroscientists are now beginning to see—by the normal workings of the mind carried to an extreme, well, then you are in a lonely minority. According to periodic surveys by Gallup and other pollsters, fully 90 percent of Americans say they have experienced such things or believe they exist.

A Window into the Workings of the Human Mind

If you take the word "normal" as characteristic of the norm or majority, then it is the superstitious and those who believe in ESP, ghosts and psychic phenomena who are normal. Most scientists and skeptics roll their eyes at such sleight of word, asserting that belief in anything for which there is no empirical evidence is a sign of mental pathology and not normalcy. But a growing number of researchers, in fields such as evolutionary psychology and neurobiology, are taking such beliefs seriously in one important sense: as a window into the workings of the human mind. The studies are an outgrowth of research on religious faith, a (nearly) human universal, and are turning out to be useful for explaining fringe beliefs, too. The emerging consensus is that belief in the supernatural seems to arise from the same mental processes that underlie everyday reasoning and perception. But while the belief in ghosts, past lives, the ability of the mind to move matter and the like originate in normal mental processes, those processes become hijacked and exaggerated, so that the result is, well, Walter Semkiw.

Raised as a Roman Catholic, Semkiw is driven by a what-if optimism. If only people could accept reincarnation, he believes, Iraq's Sunnis and Shiites might stop fighting (since they might be killing someone who was once one of them). He is dismissive of the idea that reincarnation has not been empirically proved. That was the status of everything science has since proved, be it the ability of atoms to vibrate in synchrony (the basis of the laser) or of mold to cure once-lethal infections (penicillin). Dedicated to the empirical method, Semkiw believes the world is on the brink of "a science of spirituality," he says. "I don't know how you can't believe in reincarnation. All it takes is an open mind." . . .

Yearning for a Sense of Control

The pervasiveness of belief in the supernatural and paranormal may seem odd in an age of science. But ours is also an age of anxiety, a time of economic distress and social anomie, as denizens of a mobile society are repeatedly uprooted from family and friends. Historically, such times have been marked by a surge in belief in astrology, ESP and other paranormal phenomena, spurred in part by a desperate yearning to feel a sense of control in a world spinning out of control. A study reported a few weeks ago in the journal *Science* found that people asked to recall a time when they felt a loss of control saw more patterns in random noise, perceived more conspiracies in stories they read and imagined illusory correlations in financial markets than people who were not reminded that events are sometimes beyond their control. "In the absence of perceived control, people become susceptible to detecting patterns in an effort to regain some sense of organization," says psychology researcher Bruce Hood of the University of Bristol, whose upcoming book *Supersense: Why We Believe in the Unbelievable* explores the mental processes behind belief in the paranormal. "No wonder those stock market traders are clutching their rabbit's feet"—or that psychics and the paranormal seem to be rivaling reality stars for TV hegemony ("Medium," "Psychic Kids," "Lost" and the new "Fringe" and "Eleventh Hour"). Just as great religious awakenings have coincided with tumultuous eras, so belief in the paranormal also becomes much more prevalent during social and political turmoil. Such events "lead the mind to look for explanations," says Michael Shermer, president of the Skeptics Society and author of the 1997 book *Why People Believe Weird Things.* "The mind often takes a turn toward the supernatural and paranormal," which offers the comfort that benign beings are watching over you (angels), or that you will always be connected to a larger reality beyond the woes of this world (ghosts).

As science replaces the supernatural with the natural, explaining everything from thunder and lightning to the formation of planets, many people seek another source of mystery and wonder in the world. People can get that from belief in several paranormal phenomena, but none more so than thinking they were abducted by aliens. When Susan Clancy was a graduate student in psychology at Harvard University, she was struck by how ordinary the "abductees" she was studying seemed. They were respectable, job-holding, functioning members of society, normal except for their belief that short beings with big eyes once scooped them up and took them to a spaceship. They are men like Will, a massage therapist, who was abducted repeatedly by aliens, he told Clancy, and became so close to one that their union produced twin boys whom, sadly, he never sees. Numerous studies have found that abductees are not suffering from any known mental illness. They are unusually prone to false memories, and tend to be creative, fantasy-prone and imaginative. But so are lots of people who have never met a little green man.

Abductees Share an Inability to Think Scientifically

Some 40 percent of Americans believe it's possible that aliens have grabbed some of us, polls show, compared with 25 percent in the 1980s. What makes abductees stand out is something so common, it's a wonder there aren't more of them: an inability to think scientifically. Clancy asked abductees if they understand that sleep paralysis, in which waking up during a dream causes the dream to leak into consciousness even while you remain immobilized, can produce the weird visions and helplessness that abductees describe. Of course, they say, but that doesn't apply to them. And do they understand that the most likely explanation of bad dreams, impotence, nosebleeds, loneliness, bruises or just waking up to find their pajamas on the floor does not involve aliens? Yes, they told her, but abduction feels like the best explanation. Larry, for instance, woke from a dream, saw shadowy figures around his bed and felt a stabbing pain in his groin. He ran through the possibilities—a biotech firm's stealing his sperm, angels, repressed memory of childhood sexual abuse—and only then settled on alien abduction as the most plausible. The scientific principle that the simplest explanation is most likely to be right is, well, alien to abductees. But again, an inability to think scientifically is exceedingly common. We are more irrational than we are rational; emotions drive voting behavior more strongly than analysis of candidates' records and positions does. The universal human need to find meaning and purpose in life is stronger and more basic than any attachment to empiricism, logic or objective reality.

Something as common as loneliness can draw us to the paranormal. In a study published in February, scientists induced feelings of loneliness in people by telling them that a personality questionnaire they filled out revealed that, by middle age, they would have few friends and be socially isolated. After this ruse, participants were more likely to say they believed in ghosts, angels, the Devil, miracles, curses and God than were participants who were told their future held many friendships, found Nicholas Epley, of the University of Chicago, and colleagues.

Evolving Brain Systems

That we are suckers for weird beliefs reflects the fact that the brain systems that allow and even encourage them "evolved for other things," says James Griffith, a psychiatrist and neurologist at George Washington University. A bundle of neurons in the superior parietal lobe, a region toward the top and rear of the brain, for instance, distinguishes where your body ends and the material world begins. Without it, you couldn't navigate through a door frame. But other areas of the brain, including the thinking regions in the frontal lobes, sometimes send "turn off!" signals to this structure, such as when we are falling asleep or when we feel physical communion with another person (that's a euphemism for sex). During intense prayer or meditation, brain-imaging studies show, the structure is also especially quiet. Unable to find the dividing line between self and world, the brain adapts by experiencing a sense of holism and connectedness. You feel a part of something larger than yourself. This ability to shut off the sense of where you end and the world begins, then, may promote other beliefs that bring a sense of connection, even if they involve alien kidnappers.

Other normal brain functions can be hijacked for spooky purposes, too. Neither the eyes nor the ears can take in every aspect of an object. The brain, therefore, fills in the blanks. Consider the optical illusion known as the Kanizsa triangle, in which three black Pac-Man shapes sit at what could be the corners of a triangle, their open mouths pointed inward. Almost everyone "sees" three white lines forming that triangle, but there are in fact

Cognitive Biases Are Now More Definitive

Since the early 1990s, a considerable amount of research has been carried out investigating possible cognitive biases underlying paranormal belief and experience. It is clear that a wide range of situations exist that can potentially lead people to believe that they have experienced the paranormal when in fact they have not. The question regarding possible differences between believers and non-believers in the paranormal in terms of proneness to cognitive biases can now be answered rather more definitively than was possible then. Although believers and non-believers do not seem to differ reliably in terms of critical thinking, and inconsistently reported differences in probabilistic reasoning ability may have alternative explanations, many of the other postulated cognitive biases do seem to be reliably related to paranormal belief and experience.

Christopher C. French and Krissy Wilson,
Sergio Della Sala, ed., Tall Tales About the
Mind and Brain: Separating Fact from
Fiction. *New York: Oxford University Press,*
2007.

no lines. What does the "seeing" is not the eyes but the brain, which habitually takes messy, incomplete input and turns it into a meaningful, complete picture. This drive to see even what is not objectively there is easily hijacked. "Perceptually, the world is chronically ambiguous and requires an interpretation," says Stewart Guthrie, professor emeritus of anthropology at Fordham University and author of *Faces in the Clouds*. And suddenly you see Satan in the smoke from the World Trade Center. "We see the Virgin Mary in a potato chip or Jesus on an underpass wall because we're using our existing cognitive structures to make sense of an ambiguous or amorphous stimuli," says psychologist Mark Reinecke, professor of psychiatry and behavioral sciences at Northwestern University.

Scientists mean "see" literally. Brain imaging shows that the regions that become active when people imagine seeing or hearing something are identical to those that become active when they really do see or hear something in the outside world. This holds true for schizophrenics (their visual cortex becomes active when they hallucinate people, and their auditory cortex when they hear voices, in ways that are indistinguishable from when they perceive real people and voices) and for healthy people engaging in mental imagery (think of a pink elephant). It is not too far a step for mentally healthy people to see or hear what they are thinking intensely about. Christina Puchalski, director of the George Washington Institute for Spirituality and Health, felt her dead mother's presence "with me in a very deep and profound way, emanating from a certain direction," she says. "Maybe if you're thinking very strongly about that person, your mind is creating the sense that he is there."

A more common experience is to see patterns in coincidences, something that also represents a hijacking of normal and useful brain function. You think about the girl at the party last Saturday and—bam!—she calls you. You think about the girl who chatted you up in class—and never hear from her. Guess which experience you remember? Thanks to the psychological glitch called confirmatory bias, the mind better recalls events and experiences that validate what we believe than those that refute those beliefs.

But why? Why do we remember the times we thought of someone just before she texted us and forget all the times we had no such premonition? When the mind was evolving, failing to make an association (snakes with rattles are to be avoided) could get you killed, while making a false association (dancing will make it rain) mostly just wasted time, Michael Shermer points out. "We are left with a legacy of false positives," he says. "Hallucinations become ghosts or aliens; knocking noises in an empty house indicate spirits and poltergeists; shadows and lights in a tree become the Virgin Mary."

Paranormal Beliefs Are Linked to Human Survival

The brain also evolved to recoil from danger, and the most frequent sources of danger back in the Stone Age were not guns and cars but saber-toothed tigers and other living things. As a result, we are programmed to impute vitality to even inanimate threats, as Bristol's Hood has demonstrated. When he gives a speech about irrational beliefs, he holds up an old cardigan and asks who would be willing to wear it in exchange for about $40. Usually, every hand in the audience shoots up. But when Hood adds that the sweater was once worn by a notorious murderer, almost every hand disappears. "People view evil as something physical, even tangible, and able to infect the sweater" as easily as lice, Hood says. "The idea of spirits and souls appearing in this world becomes more plausible if we believe in general that the nonphysical can transfer over to the physical world. From there it's only a small step to believing that a thunk in an empty house is a footstep."

There is a clear survival advantage to imputing aliveness and asking questions later. That's why, during human evolution, our ancestors developed what is called a hypersensitive agency-detection device, says Benson Saler, professor emeritus of anthropology at Brandeis University. This is an acute sensitivity to the presence of living beings, something we default to when what we perceive could be alive or inanimate. "Whether it's a rock formation or a hungry bear, it's better to assume it's a hungry bear," says Saler. "If you suppose it's a rock formation, and it turns out to be a hungry bear, you're not in business much longer."

Defaulting to the "it's alive!" assumption was "of such considerable value that evolution provided us with greater sensitivity to the presence of living agents than we needed," says Saler. "We respond to the slightest hint or indication of agency by assuming there are living things present. Developing ideas about ghosts and spirits is simply a derivative of this hypersensitivity to the possibility" that a living being is present, and too bad if it also produces the occasional (or even frequent) false positives.

The belief that minds are not bound to bodies, and therefore that ghosts and other spirits exist here in the physical world, reflects a deep dualism in the human psyche. No matter how many times neuroscientists assert that the mind has no existence independent of the brain, "we still think of our essence as mental, and of our mind as being independent of body," says Fordham's Guthrie. "Once you've signed on to that, existence after death is really quite natural." This dualism shows up in children as young as 2, says psychologist Paul Bloom of Yale University: kids readily believe that people can exchange bodies, for instance, and since ghosts lack material bodies but have minds and memories, belief in dualism makes them perfectly plausible. At the even more basic level of perception, the brain is wired for faces, says Northwestern's Reinecke. "Even in the first weeks of life, infants tend to perceive angles, contours and shapes that are consistent with faces," he says. There's Mary on the potato chip again.

Why Are There Skeptics?

All of which raises a question. If the brain is wired so as to make belief in the paranormal seemingly inevitable, why are there any skeptics? And not just "any," but more assertive, activist ones. Groups such as the Committee for Skeptical Inquiry, the Skeptics Society and the James Randi Educational Foundation all work to debunk claims of the paranormal. A growing number of scientists and others now proudly wear the badge of "skeptic," just as more scholars are coming out as atheists, like Richard Dawkins did in his 2006 book *The God Delusion* and as Christopher Hitchens did in his 2007 tome *God Is Not Great*. The growing numbers and assertiveness of skeptics (and public atheists) reflects the fact that they "have long felt like we belong to a beleaguered minority," says Shermer, who was once a born-again Christian. Their more aggressive attitude provides a sense of mission and community that skeptics, no less than believers, crave. It takes effort to resist the allure of belief, with its promise of fellowship, community and comfort in the face of mortality and a pointless, uncaring universe. There must be compensating rewards.

One such compensation, it is fair to say, is a feeling of intellectual superiority. It is rewarding to look at the vast hordes of believers, conclude that they are idiots and delight in the fact that you aren't. Another is that skeptics believe, or at least hope, that they can achieve at least one thing that believers seek, but without abandoning their principles. Skeptics, no less than believers, think it would be wonderful if we could speak to dead loved ones, or if we ourselves never died. But skeptics instead "seek immortality through our . . . lasting achievements," Shermer explains. "We, too, hope that our wishes for eternity might be fulfilled." Too bad that as they fight the good fight for rationality, their most powerful opponent is nothing less than the human brain.

"We are turning into a nation of mystics regardless of the frustration of organized science or organized religion. And we might add, a nation of intelligent mystics."

Higher Education Is Linked to Belief in Paranormal Phenomena

Brad Steiger

In the following viewpoint, a paranormal phenomena writer proposes that, contrary to popular assumption, education increases belief in the paranormal. A nationwide poll found that college seniors and graduate students were more inclined than freshmen to believe in telepathy, ghosts, and other paranormal concepts, he states. Furthermore, he maintains, other findings demonstrate that individuals who report seeing UFOs or aliens are no less intelligent or mentally healthy than others. In his opinion, spirituality is essential to humanity, and education should not compromise beliefs in the unknown. Brad Steiger is the author of several books on paranormal phenomena including Real Ghosts, Restless Spirits, and Haunted Places.

As you read, consider the following questions:

1. How do the figures of college seniors and graduate students who professed a belief toward the paranormal compare to freshmen, according to the author?

2. Why do skeptics find difficulty in accepting that a person can have both a higher education and beliefs in the paranormal, in the author's words?

3. As described by the author, what have researchers established about people with high degrees of psychic ability?

"Believe it or not," [science writer] Robert Roy Britt writes in the January 20, 2006 issue of *LiveScience*, "according to a new study higher education is linked to a greater tendency to believe in ghosts and other paranormal phenomena."

Even though researchers Bryan Farha at Oklahoma City University and Gary Steward of University of Central Oklahoma admitted that they had expectations of finding contrary results, their poll of college students found that seniors and graduate students were more likely to believe in haunted houses, ghosts, telepathy, spirit channeling and other paranormal phenomena than were freshmen.

Skeptics Are Confounded

Although the results of the survey are not surprising to long-time researchers in the metaphysical/psychic fields, what is startling is the fact that the poll analysis is published in the January–February [2006] issue of the *Skeptical Inquirer* magazine, the journal of true unbelievers. While the poll may have been conducted with expectations of demonstrating that as students became more educated they dropped questionable beliefs in favor of more skeptical attitudes, the *Skeptical Inquirer* must be congratulated for publishing results that they really did not wish to find.

Farha's and Steward's survey was based on a nationwide Gallup Poll in 2001 that found younger Americans more likely to believe in the paranormal than older respondents. The results of the Farha/Steward poll discovered that gaining more education was not a guarantee of skepticism or disbelief toward the paranormal. While only 23% of the freshmen quizzed professed a belief toward paranormal concepts, the figures rose to 31% for college seniors and 34% for graduate students.

The complete results of the survey may be found in the January–February issue of the *Skeptical Inquirer*. The percentages are rounded, and I have indicated the Gallup Poll 2001 figures in parenthesis. . . .

Belief in psychic/spiritual healing: 56 (54)

Belief in ESP: 28 (50)

Haunted houses: 40 (42)

Demonic possession: 40 (41)

Ghosts/spirits of the dead: 39 (38)

Telepathy: 24 (36)

Extraterrestrials visited Earth in the past: 17 (33)

Clairvoyance and prophecy: 24 (32)

Communication with the dead: 16 (28)

Astrology: 17 (28)

Witches: 26 (26)

Reincarnation: 14 (25)

Channeling: 10 (15)

It is in the "Not Sure" column that the researchers found that the higher the education level achieved, the more likelihood there was of believing in paranormal dimensions and the possibilities of a broader spectrum of reality.

Belief in psychic/spiritual healing: 26 (19)

Belief in ESP: 39 (20)

Haunted houses: 25 (16)

Demonic possession: 28 (16)

Ghosts/spirits of the dead: 27 (17)

Telepathy: 34 (26)

Extraterrestrials visited Earth in the past: 34 (27)

Clairvoyance and prophecy: 33 (23)

Communication with the dead: 29 (26)

Astrology: 26 (18)

Witches: 19 (15)

Reincarnation: 28 (20)

Channeling: 29 (21)

Why Do Skeptics Disbelieve?

Why do skeptics find it so difficult to believe that individuals who achieve a higher education may still maintain a belief in the paranormal? The world of the paranormal is one where effect often precedes cause, where mind often influences matter, where individuals communicate over great distances without physical aids, and where the spiritual essence of those deceased may be seen. Why, especially in an age of new theories embracing quantum physics and other dimensions, should skeptics find it difficult to believe in a world that lies beyond the five senses and the present reach of science?

For those of us who have been researching and writing in the paranormal, UFO, and spiritual fields for many years, the repeated allegation that we and our readers must be undereducated and unaware of the science and technology of our contemporary culture becomes very annoying. As early as 1965, when I was researching *ESP: Your Sixth Sense*—which, in addition to becoming a popular book became a college and high school text, complete with workbook and study guide—the pioneering work of Dr. Gardner Murphy, Dr. Montague Ullman, Dr. Stanley Krippner, Dr. Henry Margenau, and many others had already demonstrated that contrary to common assumption, intelligence has little connection to paranormal abilities or beliefs. Neither is it the "odd" or poorly adjusted members of society who most often demonstrate high degrees of psychic ability. Quite the contrary

Opening the Door to Pseudoscience Speculation

Our own era has seen space travel, in vitro fertilization, cloning, and the Internet. Next to these feats, alien visitation may seem more credible. Only more meticulous knowledge of the scientific and technological processes that make "speaking over wires" or air travel possible may allow adults to distinguish between what is viable and what is not. Thus, even among members of the general public with high levels of education, science discovery or applications may open the doors to pseudoscience speculation.

S.C. Losh, C.M. Tavani, R. Njoroge,
R. Wilke, and M. McAuley, "What Does
Education Really Do? Educational Dimensions
and Pseudo Science Support in the American
Public, 1979–2001," Skeptical Inquirer,
September–October 2003.

appears to be true. Those individuals who are well-adjusted socially and who are possessed of an extraverted rather than an introverted personality are the ones who score consistently higher in ESP tests.

The January 12, 1994 issue of *USA Today* carried the results of a survey conducted by Jeffrey S. Levin, associate professor at Eastern Virginia Medical School, Norfolk, which stated that more than two-thirds of the U.S. population has had at least one mystical experience. Furthermore, Levin said, although only 5% of the population have such experiences often, such mystical encounters "seem to be getting more common with each successive generation." And very interestingly, Levin added, individuals active in mainstream churches or synagogues report fewer mystical experiences than the general population.

The November 1993 issue of the *Journal of Abnormal Psychology* announced the finds of psychologists at Carleton University of Ottawa, that people who report seeing a UFO or an alien are not any less intelligent or psychologically healthy than other people. Their findings clearly contradicted the previously held notions that people who seemingly have bizarre experiences, such as missing time and communicating with aliens, have "wild imaginations and are easily swayed into believing the unbelievable."

Dr. Nicholas P. Spanos, who led the study and administered a battery of psychological tests to a large number of UFO experiencers, said that such individuals were not at all "off the wall." On the contrary, he stated, "They tend to be white-collar, relatively well-educated representatives of the middle class."

Paranormal Experiences Are Becoming More Common

Psychiatrists Colin Ross and Shaun Joshi have affirmed that paranormal experiences have become so common in the general population that "no theory of normal psychology which does not take them into account can be comprehensive."

It may well be that we are turning into a nation of mystics regardless of the frustration of organized science or organized religion. And we might add, a nation of intelligent mystics.

The October 27, 2004 issue of *USA Today* declared that "a spiritually inclined student is a happier student." According to a national study of students conducted by the Higher Education Research Institute at the University of California, Los Angeles, being spiritual contributes to one's sense of psychological well-being.

"A high degree of spirituality correlates with high self-esteem and feeling good about the way life is headed," Sarah Hofius wrote of the study that took place at forty-six wide-ranging universities and colleges, encompassing 3,680 third-year students. "The study defines spirituality as desiring to integrate spirituality into one's life, believing that we are all spiritual beings, believing in the sacredness of life and having spiritual experiences."

Another survey that should have offered an enormous amount of proof that one can achieve a higher education and still believe in the paranormal was released on December 20, 2004, revealing that 74% of medical doctors believe that miracles have occurred in the past and 73% believe that miracles can occur to-day. Sixty-seven percent of the doctors encouraged their patients to pray; 59% admitted that they prayed for their patients.

The national survey, conducted by HCD Research and the Louis Finkelsten Institute for Religious and Social Studies of the Jewish Theological Seminary, polled 1,100 physicians through-out the United States. According to Dr. Alan Mittleman, Director of the Finkelstein Institute, doctors "although presumably more highly educated than their average patient, are not necessarily more secular or radically different in religious outlook." Perhaps because of their frequent involvement with matters of life and death, medical doctors do not lose their belief in the miraculous as their level of education increases.

Blending Paranormal Beliefs with Skepticism

In 2002, the National Science Foundation found that 60% of adults in the United States agreed or strongly agreed that some people possessed psychic powers or extrasensory perception (ESP). In June 2002, the Consumer Analysis Group conducted the most extensive survey ever done in the United Kingdom and revealed that 67% of adults believed in psychic powers and that two out of three surveyed believed in an afterlife.

Michael Shermer, the ubiquitous talking head who represents the skeptical view in dozens of television documentaries each year, author of *Why People Believe Weird Things* and editor of the aforementioned the *Skeptical Inquirer*, was among those who deplored the findings that such a high percentage of Americans accepted the reality of ESP. In Shermer's analysis, such statistics posed a serious problem for science educators. Complaining that people too readily accepted the claims of pseudoscience, Shermer concluded his regular column for *Scientific American* by stating that "for those lacking a fundamental comprehension of how science works, the siren song of pseudoscience becomes too alluring to resist, not matter how smart you are."

Shermer must have been somewhat surprised some years earlier when he interviewed Martin Gardner, the prolific science writer, author of the classic *Fads and Fallacies in the Name of Science*, and the founder of the modern skeptical movement, who told him that he believed in God, that he sometimes prayed and worshipped, and that he hoped for life after death. Gardner explained that he called himself a "philosophical theist, or sometimes a fideist, who believes something on the basis of emotional reasons, rather than intellectual reasons."

Gardner also identified himself as a "mysterian," explaining that "there are certain things I regard as ultimate mysteries. Free will is one of those. Another is time. Time and space are the ultimate mysteries. Free will is bound up in the mysteries of time about which we can never understand, at least at this stage of evolutionary history."

In my opinion, humankind's one truly essential factor is its spirituality. The artificial concepts to which we have given the designation of sciences are no truer in the ultimate sense than dreams, visions, and inspirations. The quest for absolute proof or objective truth may always be unattainable when it seeks to define and limit the Soul. And I truly believe that one can achieve a high level of education and still maintain a firm belief in the unseen world.

"People want to believe, and most simply can't help it."

A Variety of Factors May Influence Belief in Paranormal Phenomena

Robert Roy Britt

In the following viewpoint, a science editor proposes that the prevalence of paranormal beliefs can be attributed to several factors. He claims that the supernatural was first invoked before the discoveries of modern science provided explanations for occurrences beyond human control. As for the influence of religion on believing in the paranormal, studies have turned up contradictory findings, he contends. However, education increases paranormal beliefs, he maintains, as does the promotion of monsters, ghosts, and psychics in the media. Robert Roy Britt is editorial director of Imaginova, a digital media and commerce company focused on science.

As you read, consider the following questions:

1. In Britt's opinion, what is harder to believe than monsters?
2. What instance does Britt provide of belief in curses crossing with religion?

3. How does the author characterize the depiction of the paranormal in the media?

Monsters are everywhere these days, and belief in them is as strong as ever. What's harder to believe is why so many people buy into hazy evidence, shady schemes and downright false reports that perpetuate myths that often have just one ultimate truth: They put money in the pockets of their purveyors.

The bottom line, according to several interviews with people who study these things: People want to believe, and most simply can't help it.

"Many people quite simply just want to believe," said Brian Cronk, a professor of psychology at Missouri Western State University. "The human brain is always trying to determine why things happen, and when the reason is not clear, we tend to make up some pretty bizarre explanations."

A related question: Does belief in the paranormal have anything to do with religious belief?

The answer to that question is decidedly nuanced, but studies point to an interesting conclusion: People who practice religion are typically encouraged not to believe in the paranormal, but rather to put their faith in one deity, whereas those who aren't particularly active in religion are more free to believe in Bigfoot or consult a psychic.

"Christians and New Agers, paranormalists, etc. all have one thing in common: a spiritual orientation to the world," said sociology Professor Carson Mencken of Baylor University.

The Paranormal Appeals to the Public

A tale last week [in August 2008] by three men who said they have remains of Bigfoot in a freezer was reported by many Web sites as anywhere from final proof of the creature to at least a very compelling case to keep the fantasy ball rolling and cash registers ringing for Bigfoot trinkets and tourism (all three men involved make money off the belief in this creature). Even mainstream media treated a Friday press conference about the "finding" as news.

Reactions by the public ranged from skeptical curiosity to blind faith.

"I believe they do exist but I'm not sure about this," said one reader reacting to a story on *LiveScience* that cast doubt the claim. "I guess we will find out . . . if this is on the up and up," wrote another. "However, that said, I know they exist."

A subsequent test on the supposed Bigfoot found nothing but the DNA of humans and an opossum, a small, cat-like creature.

Also last week, in Texas there was yet another sensational yet debunkable sighting of chupacabra, a beast of Latin-American folklore. The name means "goat sucker." In this case, law enforcement bought into the hooey with an apparent wink and nod.

Ellie Carter, a patrol trainee with the DeWitt County sheriff's office, saw the beast and was, of course, widely quoted. "It was this—thing, looking right at us," she said "I think that's a chupacabra!" After watching a video of the beast taken by a sheriff's deputy, biologist Scott Henke of Texas A&M University said, "It's a dog for sure," according to a story on *Scientific American's* Web site.

Meanwhile, the sheriff did nothing to tamp down rampant speculation, expressing delight that he might have a monster on his hands. "I love this for DeWitt County," said Sheriff Jode Zavesky, who would presumably be just as thrilled to let Dracula or a werewolf run free.

With that kind of endorsement and the human propensity to believe in just about anything, it's clear that Bigfoot and chupacabra are just two members in a cast of mythical characters and dubious legends and ideas will likely never go away.

In a 2006 study, researchers found a surprising number of college students believe in psychics, witches, telepathy, channeling and a host of other questionable ideas. A full 40 percent said they believe houses can be haunted.

Why are people so eager to accept flimsy and fabricated evidence in support of unlikely and even outlandish creatures and ideas? Why is the paranormal realm, from psychic predictions to UFO sightings, so alluring to so many?

Paranormal Beliefs Are Part of Human Nature

Since people have been people, experts figure, they have believed in the supernatural, from gods to ghosts and now every sort of monster in between.

"While it is difficult to know for certain, the tendency to believe in the paranormal appears to be there from the beginning," explained Christopher Bader, a Baylor sociologist and colleague of Mencken. "What changes is the content of the paranormal. For example, very few people believe in faeries and elves these days. But as belief in faeries faded, other beliefs, such as belief in UFOs, emerged to take their place."

Figuring out why people are this way is a little trickier.

"It is an artifact of our brain's desire to find cause and effect," Cronk, the psychology professor, said in an email interview. "That ability to predict the future is what makes humans 'smart' but it also has side effects like superstitions [and] belief in the paranormal."

"Humans first started believing in the supernatural because they were trying to understand things they couldn't explain," says Benjamin Radford, a book author, paranormal investigator and managing editor of *Skeptical Inquirer* magazine. "It's basically the same process as mythology: At one point people didn't understand why the sun rose and set each day, so they suggested that a chariot pulled the sun across the heavens."

Before modern scientific explanations of germ theory, explained Radford, who writes the "Bad Science" column for *LiveScience*, people didn't understand how diseases could travel from one person to another. "They didn't understand why a child was stillborn, or why a drought occurred, so they came to believe that such events had supernatural causes," he said.

"All societies have invoked the supernatural to explain things beyond their control and understanding, especially good and bad events," Radford said. "In many places—even today—people believe that disasters or bad luck is caused by witches or curses."

Which raises the bigger question: With science having answered so many questions in the past couple centuries, why do paranormal beliefs remain so strong?

Religion's Influence on Paranormal Beliefs

Sometimes the belief in curses crosses paths with religion, as was the case in 2005 when televangelist John Hagee (whose endorsement was solicited and received by presidential hopeful John McCain) blamed Hurricane Katrina on God's wrath for a gay parade that had been scheduled for the Monday of the storm's arrival.

"I believe that New Orleans had a level of sin that was offensive to God, and they are—were recipients of the judgment of God for that," Hagee said at the time, reiterating the belief in 2006.

That might lead one to assume religion and paranormal beliefs are intertwined.

But in a 2004 survey, the researchers at Baylor found just the opposite.

"Paranormal beliefs are very strongly *negatively* related to religious belief," study team member Rod Stark said this week.

Another study, of 391 U.S. college students done in 2000, found that participants who did not believe in Protestant doctrine were most likely to believe in reincarnation, contact with the dead, UFOs, telepathy, prophecy, psychokinesis, or healing. Believers were the least likely to buy into the paranormal. "This may partly reflect opinions of Christians in the samples who take biblical sanctions against many 'paranormal' activities seriously," the Wheaton College researchers wrote.

Cronk, the psychologist, did a small survey of 80 college students and found no connection between religiosity and paranormal belief.

Society Influences Paranormal Beliefs

Public opinion surveys indicate that the overwhelming majority of Americans believe some paranormal claims. At the same time, most specific beliefs are minority viewpoints. This may indicate low exposure rates to particular claims, but it seems unlikely given the high profile of so many paranormal claims and claimants. It is more likely that most people are cognizant of the marginal status of these claims but hesitant to accept them without social support. Our evidence suggests that such cautiousness results in a degree of resistance to social influence—not a high degree, necessarily, but enough to stave off beliefs in claims at the "wilder" end of the plausibility spectrum, at least until the needed social support is perceived to be in place. That support may originate in the strength, immediacy, or number of real or imagined reference groups, or in networks of significant others—family, friends, work colleagues, and so forth. Our findings also suggest that paranormal claims endorsed by proximal, legitimate, higher-status others are especially contagious.

Barry N. Markovsky and Shane R. Thye,
"Social Influence on Paranormal Beliefs,"
Sociological Perspectives, *vol. 44, no. 1,*
Spring 2001.

But a 2002 study in Canada did find a correlation between religious beliefs and paranormal beliefs, Cronk notes. He figures that among other explanations, Canadians may not have the same belief systems as U.S. residents.

"My guess is that religiosity has a lot to do with how you were raised, and less to do with genetics," Cronk said. "Those people who may have a high genetic susceptibility to 'faith-based knowledge' may end up being highly religious or may end up having belief in the paranormal depending on how they were raised. Those people less susceptible to that method of forming beliefs may still end up being highly religious if they were raised in a religious family."

The Highly Religious Are Not Paranormal Believers

Mencken, the Baylor sociologist, says sacrifice and stigma (for holding ideas outside the group norm) keep the paranormal at bay among the highly religious. He has two papers forthcoming that are based on a national survey of 1,700 people.

The first, to be published in the journal *Sociology of Religion* in 2009, reveals this:

"Among Christians, those who attend church very often (and are exposed to stigma and sacrifice within their congregations) are least likely to believe it the paranormal," Mencken told *LiveScience*. "Conversely, those Christians who do not attend church very often (maybe once or twice a year) are the most likely to hold paranormal beliefs."

A third group, which he calls naturalists, do not hold supernatural views, Christian or paranormal.

Another study to published in December in the *Review of Religious Research*, shows that those who go to church "are much less likely to consult horoscopes, visit psychics, purchase New Age items," and so on, Mencken said. "However, among those Christians who do not attend church, there is a much higher level of participation in these phenomena."

Profiling Paranormal Believers Is Difficult

Profiling the typical Bigfoot believer turns out to be as challenging as determining the scientific methodology of a psychic, however.

"Perhaps amazingly, [paranormal beliefs] are not related at all to education," Stark said. "Ph.D.s are as likely as high school dropouts to believe in Bigfoot, Loch Ness Monster, ghosts, etc."

The 2006 study of college students, done by Bryan Farha at Oklahoma City University and Gary Steward Jr. of the University of Central Oklahoma, reached a similar conclusion. Belief in the paranormal—from astrology to communicating with the dead—increases during college, rising from 23 percent among freshmen to 31 percent in seniors and 34 percent among graduate students.

Bader, the sociologist at Baylor, and his colleagues teamed up with the Gallup organization to conduct a national survey of 1,721 people in 2005 and found nearly 30 percent think it is possible to influence the physical world through the mind alone (another 30 percent were undecided on that point). More than 20 percent figure it's possible to communicate with the dead. Nearly 40 percent believe in haunted houses.

Asked if "creatures such as Bigfoot and the Loch Ness Monster will one day be discovered by science," 18.8 percent agreed while 25.9 percent were undecided.

In a remote Himalayan village, on the other hand, belief in Bigfoot's cousin, the yeti, is seen by some as a sign of ignorance.

The Media Promotes the Paranormal

Today's ubiquitous and often one-sided, promotional coverage of the paranormal, both on the Internet and TV, perpetuate myths and folklore as well or better than any ancient storyteller. Fiction and belief masquerade as fact and news, feeding the 24/7 appetite of the easily swayed.

Scientists are left with an impossible task: proving something does not exist. You can prove a rock is there. You can't prove that Bigfoot or a ghost or the god of thunder is not there. Bigfoot paraphernalia purveyors and cash-cow psychics know this well.

"Many paranormalists claim that their powers only work sometimes, or that they don't work if there is a 'non-believer' in the room," Cronk points out.

Or, in the case of the unsupportive DNA testing on Bigfoot last week, the top proponent, Tom Biscardi (who recently produced a film about Bigfoot and might be said to have an interest in garnering press coverage) simply dodged the mythbusting bullet by claiming the DNA samples might have been contaminated.

Money motivates even the law to look the other way.

Regarding the chupacabra "sighting" last week in Cuero, Texas: "It's amazing," said Zavesky, DeWitt County sheriff. "We still don't know what it is."

Of course his county, specifically the town of Cuero, has been dubbed the Chupacabra Capital of the World and benefits by monster tourism.

So while a sheriff might well be concerned if he thinks there's a goat-sucking menace in town, Zavesky is in no hurry to catch the beast and debunk the myth. "It has brought a lot of attention to us," he said. "We're not near ready to put this one to bed yet."

> *"If we don't speak out to the television networks or question the actions of the local paranormal advocates, then we can only expect the paranormal to become ever more normal."*

Paranormal Reality Television Shows Encourage Belief in Paranormal Phenomena

Sharon Hill

In the following viewpoint, a paranormal skeptic argues that programming on television rationalizes and spreads belief in the supernatural. She claims that even before the rise of paranormal reality TV, a study showed that watching ghost-hunting shows is related to belief in such phenomena. In the author's view, paranormal investigations are based on false science and their influence on the public must be countered. Sharon Hill is the founder of Doubtful News, *a blog on skepticism.*

As you read, consider the following questions:

1. What happens if one buys into the idea that paranormal phenomena are real, in Hill's opinion?

2. What examples does the author offer of the influence of television ghost hunters on their fans?

3. How can misinformation from paranormal television be addressed, as suggested by Hill?

U.K. researcher and psychology professor Richard Wiseman has explained very well that those who believe in the paranormal will report more paranormal experiences than those who do not believe. If you buy into the idea that a paranormal phenomenon is real, and deliberately search for it, then find it you will. Everything odd that happens in that dark cemetery, creaky old home, or dilapidated, abandoned hospital will feed into your paranormal mindset. If you think your instruments record ghostly activity, then you see the fluctuating measurements as evidence ghosts are there. If you believe spirits can influence recording equipment, then you will hear their disembodied voices in EVPs [electronic voice phenomenon]. So it is not a surprise to find viewers imitate their favorite ghost hunters from TV and get similar results. In 2001, a study concluded that paranormal television viewing is related to the viewers' belief in the paranormal. This was done BEFORE the boom in "reality" ghost hunting shows. As far as I know, no studies have assessed how the widespread media portrayal of real-life ghost hunting influences people's belief in the reality of these phenomena. Or, worse, what if the viewers think that what ghost hunters do is valid and "scientific?"

Sure, many tune in to shows like *Ghost Hunters* and *Ghost Adventures* just to laugh at a bunch of people going around scaring themselves but a good portion of the fans of these shows DO think it's real. Pay a visit to their fan forums or go to their public appearances if you doubt it. Paranormal investigation groups openly state they are inspired and influenced to do what they do by watching TV ghost hunters. They will affiliate themselves with TAPS (The Atlantic Paranormal Society [*Ghost*

Hunters]) or GAC (Ghost Adventure Crew) as a symbol of their legitimacy.

One paranormal-related news story (among the hundreds this time of year) particularly caught my attention as an example of the influence of TV: Kansas man takes up ghost hunting. He admits what hooked him, ". . . he started thinking he could do what he was watching on cable."

The article also notes: "Like those investigation teams on television, the team has recorded unexplainable videos and 'EVPs' . . ." and "The EMF detector was showing a magnetic field, and the homeowners had suspected there was the spirit of a woman in the house."

Paranormal Phenomena Have Become Mainstream

Television and the internet have spread these paranormal-related memes efficiently, haven't they? Has it become mainstream and acceptable to be a paranormal investigator? If not, it's close to it. The popularity of paranormal reality TV has not abated.

Research studies tell us that interest and belief in the paranormal are related to people's personal experiences. A casual review of the biographies of MOST of today's pro-paranormal investigators bears this out. It is no different than the man profiled in the above report. He is looking for answers to questions that persist as unanswered to him.

While mainstream science does not count paranormal phenomena as genuine (it can't really, since science builds conclusions upon what we provisionally know, not WISH, to be true), today's ghost investigators treat the paranormal as if it is some fringe area of nature left for intrepid amateurs to unlock via gadgetry.

They use seriously sciencey sounding explanations—all bogus. There is no scientific evidence for ghosts as remnants of the now dead. There is, however, a scientific explanation for what people experience as ghosts. It's in our brains, it's in our psyche.

Sadly, that internal explanation hasn't been quite as popular as the spookier idea of external entities.

Ghost hunting shows on television justify and enhance belief in the paranormal. They feed it. Often the audience members eating it up are children and teens. Frankly, the only way to address such misinformation is to hit it head on. General science education isn't going to be an immediate help. In order to make an impact, we must address the subject specifically. This means greater media coverage of a skeptical viewpoint, college (or free) classes in how to evaluate paranormal claims, public challenging of the "paranormal experts" to defend their conclusions. It won't eliminate the belief in the paranormal explanations, of course, but just as TV has made a difference to enhance belief, advocacy of the non-paranormal view may help to dispel some of it.

I get excited every time I find a story for *Doubtful News* that I can label "Skeptical Activism." If we don't speak out to the television networks or question the actions of the local paranormal advocates, then we can only expect the paranormal to become ever more normal—mainstream and accepted.

> "Paranormal reality TV—an American
> contribution to entertainment
> culture—is now the interlocutor
> around new ideas regarding history,
> spirituality, science, and cultural
> identity."

Paranormal Reality Television Shows Reflect Cultural Issues

Deonna Kelli Sayed

In the following viewpoint, a paranormal investigator contends that the popularity of paranormal television is tied to societal and cultural change. Following the 9/11 attacks, ghost-hunting shows allow Americans to mourn and cope with the trauma and unknown threats of terrorism, she explains. Furthermore, the author maintains, paranormal television challenges established discourses on science and history by drawing from religion, folklore, and individual experience. She deduces that such programming encourages audiences to shape their own understanding of the world. Deonna Kelli Sayed is the author of Paranormal Obsession: America's Fascination with Ghosts, Hauntings, Spooks, and Spirits.

As you read, consider the following questions:

1. As stated by Sayed, how does paranormal television "function to make history right"?
2. In what ways does paranormal television present the concepts of good and evil and free will, in Sayed's view?
3. How do ghost-hunting television shows challenge history, as claimed by Sayed?

Paranormal reality TV is about more than ghosts and spooky experiences. Such programming is an American story attempting to define our existence at a post–9/11, globalized cultural moment. Ghost reports have historically increased during times of cultural and social change. With this in mind, paranormal reality TV—an American contribution to entertainment culture—is now the interlocutor around new ideas regarding history, spirituality, science, and cultural identity.

Ghost hunting is not really about spirits. The shows are about the living.

SyFy launched *Ghost Hunters* in October 2004, featuring members of The Atlantic Paranormal Society (TAPS), a paranormal investigation group that has been in existence since the early 1990s. By Season Two, *Ghost Hunters* was SyFy's flagship show, and is now in its seventh season.

A couple years later in 2007, A&E's *Paranormal State* debuted. *Ghost Hunters* featured a "debunking, scientific approach." *Paranormal State* highlighted the role of story, the influence of psychical research, and prioritized client experiences. The two shows differed in style and methodology yet both provided a substantial boost to America's fascination and comfort level with ghostly occurrences. The initial wave of paranormal reality TV is now shifting due to the cancellations or discontinuation of several shows. However, the genre appears to now be an established entertainment offering regardless of its growing pains.

The immediate public response to paranormal reality TV was an exponential increase in the number of people conducting investigations or seeking a haunted experience. "Paratainment" is now [a] profitable way for the public to engage ghostly interest. Historic locations charge for investigations and events. Paranormal interest often provides much needed revenue for restoration and operational expenses. Furthermore, there are now thousands of Meetup.com and Facebook groups hosting public paranormal events, and para-themed conferences and conventions take place all over the United States. The international broadcast of the shows is encouraging a global rise in paranormal investigation. There are teams in places such as Malaysia, Israel, and Afghanistan, for example.

Paranormal TV Influences Society

The most obvious meaning behind the shows' success is that many people do accept the idea of ghosts. The most exhaustive research on American beliefs in the paranormal is from the 2005 Baylor Religion Survey. Out of 3,000 participants, 37 percent believe places can be haunted, while 20 percent feel that they have had a personal ghost experience. Sociologists discuss the results from the poll in the insight[ful] book, *Paranormal America: Ghost Encounters, UFO Sightings, Big Foot Hunts, and Other Curiosities in Religion and Culture.*

But ghosts aside, the shows have profound meaning for our national identity.

American production companies first considered paranormal-themed reality TV due to the success of the United Kingdom's *Most Haunted*. The show, which debuted in 2002, was a massive British hit. However, the American entertainment industry felt that the events of 9/11 were too raw for American audiences to engage the intimacies of ghost hunting at that time.

A few years later, however, the timing was perfect. The shows emerged to provide fascinating insight into that particular cultural moment.

The work of Dr. Jessica O'Hara in *The Philosophy of Horror* illustrates how paranormal reality TV delves into the narratives of mourning. Since that horrible event, she writes "history has presented itself as trauma, which invites us to imagine history's task as uncovering and authenticating sites of disturbance and tragedy, the haunts of restless spirits."

Ghost hunting shows allow Americans to mourn and reassemble time, as well as history, back into something we can control. As O'Hara suggests, history is now presented as trauma since 9/11. The shows work to acknowledge the departed and mourn the dead. In many ways, televised investigation also seeks to put time back into order again. In the confusing world of post–9/11 where public space is compromised by terror threats, economic instability, and unemployment, the private space of home becomes our sanctuary. Yet, even those spaces are haunted. It is in our homes where we now negotiate the relationship with the "Other" (the foreigner, the immigrant, the terrorist) through the metaphor of hauntings.

This metaphor is not a casual one. In the summer of 2009, Lowe's Home Improvement store had [a] theatrical commercial spoofing *Ghost Hunters*. The segment featured a couple in a house "that is trying to kill them." Possessed appliances and a maniacal flooded basement are on the attack. The camera then pans to a Lowe's employee saying, "Hello, my name is Doug. I work at Lowe's, and I'm here to help." His dress, body language, and verbiage is homage to *Ghost Hunter's* lead investigator, Jason Hawes, who often greets a client saying, "Hi, We're from TAPS, and we are here to help." . . .

In many ways, the shows function to make history right, at least, metaphorically. *Paranormal State* illustrates this best with the emphasis on empowering the client, who is (sometimes) an active participant in the investigation. The show also prioritizes a homeowner's emotional relationship to the haunting. All shows function to rectify the fear factor associated with the paranormal, where the ultimate goal is to make a client (and the viewer) *feel* less haunted.

Paranormal TV Eases the Fear of the Unknown

Ghost shows also placate the fear and curiosity of the unseen. We are reminded daily that we are at war against terror and this remains undefined, invisible, and unpredictable. Terrorism can strike and any moment with no advanced warning. Citizens must be on alert at all times for suspicious behavior. Yet, no clear individual or group is identified as being the source of this fear. We are not sure about who comprises al-Qaeda, thus the move to profile all Muslims and others of Middle Eastern descent. American troops are in Afghanistan and Iraq, yet the reasons for being there are contested and unclear to everyday citizens. At this point, America is at war with a "haunting." The enemy is a scary specter, and these shows provide an opportunity to make sense of and engage with this unknown.

While the United States battles an invisible evil with the War on Terror, the shows allow us to flesh out larger philosophical issues around that concept, as well as the discussion of free will. O'Hara points out that these shows promote the idea of real demons and evil entities that bother humans and sometimes oppress other spirits. *Ghost Hunters* once featured a case where they claimed a human entity was acting demonic in order to scare the family. On one level, this assertion defies logic. How can any person know what a ghost is thinking when it is hard to even prove the existence of one? Yet, the idea that a ghost would desire to behave demonically suggests the living and spiritual world is embroiled in a battle between good and evil. Likewise, this assumption surmises ghosts have free will to behave as they chose.

Negotiating between good and evil, according to the shows, is something individuals do regarding the paranormal. We hear that playing with Ouija boards is bad. Clients are sometimes told a dysfunctional home and drug or alcohol abuse can attract negative energy. Therefore, we are agents in this battle, and our free will determines the outcome. With the shows, of course, good always triumphs over evil. Cleansings and blessings are performed with great results. Clients can merely ask or demand a ghost to leave or quiet down, and the spirit can decide whether to consent. Homeowners are also reminded that whatever is present will not hurt them nor does it intend any harm. Free will and good versus evil are negotiated on every episode of paranormal reality TV.

Paranormal TV Represents Postmodernism

Paranormal reality TV is some of the most postmodern, anti-authoritarian programming on TV, and that is probably why so many find it fascinating. It is telling a new story of who we are at this cultural moment.

There are many meanings for *postmodern*, but I am going to stick with what is relevant to this discussion, with the help of the Merriam-Webster Online Dictionary. Postmodernism is "relating to, or being a theory that involves a radical reappraisal of modern assumptions about culture, identity, history, or language." This means that we can question long-held assumed Truths (like if Science really knows everything). It means we can bring historically marginalized voices into being (like a feminist retelling of history, which becomes *herstory*). Postmodernism makes novels like Dan Brown's *DaVinci Code* popular because it refutes the formal version of religious history, that of a male God, and brings in alternative perspectives. History and Authority (with a capital A) are questioned, and the role of personal and private experience carries as much weight as objective scientific evidence. Postmodernism insists on mixing familiar symbols and their meanings to create something completely new. It is very much about going beyond the cliché. The postmodern is a pastiche allowing us to reexamine what and how we know and understand commonly held assumptions about the world and ourselves.

Paranormal reality TV challenges the privileged discourse of science. All shows take assumptions from different religious, scientific, and cultural traditions and merge them into a type of pastiche theory used to explain the paranormal.

Here is a hypothetical example (this did not happen on any particular show): there is a direct-response EMF [electromagnetic field], as well as EVP [electronic voice phenomenon], captured during an investigation. The EVP says, "Help me!" Someone will submit a "scientific" hypothesis about EMF and paranormal activity, while another will recommend a cleansing ceremony to help the spirit cross over. In one sweep, science and the spiritual join to create a little truth about the paranormal. No one can argue that this analysis [is] right and no one can argue that it is wrong. The shows inform us that there are no experts in the field. Like postmodernism, the paranormal has no grand authority. Anyone can assert any truth and there are few ways to refute it. You can be a parapsychologist with a PhD, or a plumber—each has an equally valid role in this endeavor. A modern-day myth is created as the shows reassemble perspectives from science, religion, folklore, and personal experience to function as truth. In this process, they validate the way we view the world as well as our place in it. The funny thing is that the shows never provide a real answer or final resolution. Regardless of the activity featured on the episode, we never really know who or what is behind the haunting.

In many episodes, there is never a forever resolution to the haunting. The lack of a clear solution is something that reflects our own postmodern identity. As individuals, we are never completed projects, and the metaphorical ghosts that haunt us never actually materialize. Or, if they do materialize, do they ever go away?

The shows also tear down big history by prioritizing local histories, particularly those of the departed. Postmodernism allows silenced voices, like those of women and minorities, to finally speak back to a history that often excluded their stories. Investigators do what has been thought to be impossible: they allow the dead to utter injustices, losses, or grievances. The majority EVP sessions begin by asking, "Is there anyone here who would like to communicate with us?" or "Can you give us a sign of your presence?" When an EVP is captured, this prioritizes the property's history over an official version. There are real cases where captured evidence encourages fresh avenues of historical research. This sometimes forces new questions to be asked, and may unveil previously unknown information about a location.

A New Form of Spirituality Emerges

The paranormal allows a collage-type of spirituality to compensate for what many are no longer getting from religious institutions. Australian scholar Em McAvan names this as the "postmodern sacred." This new type of spirituality is inspired by science fiction, horror, and fantasy pop culture through movies like *The Matrix* trilogy, the *Harry Potter* series, *The X-files*, and paranormal reality TV. These shows and movies attach new meanings to religious symbols and ideas without consulting established religious discourse.

The individual (paranormal) experience is the "sole arbitrator of truth and authority," writes McEwan. Affirmed are the rights of ghosts—no longer does the living have sole authority to write history. Science is embraced, yet constantly challenged, through paranormal realities. These shows may engage Christian concepts of free will and good versus evil, but they also dispute traditionally held assumptions of God and theology.

Author Jeff Belanger agrees. He shares an enlightening experience, "A few years ago, I was out with some paranormal investigators somewhere. I was at a cemetery or something. Then it hit me! I had a 'holy crap!' moment. I realized this was church for these people. This was where they were getting their spiritual experience," Jeff details.

The media component creates a postmodern sacred, and embraces larger cultural issues in ways few TV programs do. Paranormal reality TV takes everything we know about [the] world—science, Truth, and ourselves—and throws it out. These larger concepts are reassembled, and a new truth is asserted.

These shows encourage us to mold the world in way to reflect who we really are at this cultural moment.

Periodical and Internet Sources Bibliography

The following articles have been selected to supplement the diverse views presented in this chapter.

Gary M. Bakker — "Paranormal Beliefs and Insight," *Skeptical Inquirer*, January–February 2011.

Courtney Bell and Harvey Richman — "Paranormal Beliefs Then and Now," *North American Journal of Psychology*, March 2012.

David Briggs — "The Complicated Connection Between Religion and the Paranormal," *Huffington Post*, February 6, 2011.

Kristen Campbell — "Not All Belief in Paranormal Phenomena Is Created Equal," *Baptist Standard*, November 7, 2008.

Erich Goode — "Why Is Creationism a Paranormal Belief?," *Psychology Today*, March 8, 2012.

Bruce Hood, interviewed by Gilbert Cruz — "Why We're Superstitious," *Time*, April 10, 2009.

David Klinghoffer — "Ghosts, Aliens, and Us," *Los Angeles Times*, December 8, 2008.

Emily Sohn — "Superstitious Beliefs Getting More Common," *Discovery News*, October 29, 2010.

Shelbi Thomas — "The Truth Is Out There," *Iowa Alumni Magazine*, August 2011.

Richard Wiseman — "Common Brain Mechanisms Underlie Supernatural Perceptions," *Scientific American Mind*, January 2012.

OPPOSING
VIEWPOINTS®
SERIES

CHAPTER 3

Are Paranormal Investigations and Practices Legitimate?

Chapter Preface

Derived from the ancient Greek words *kryptos* (hidden), *zoon* (animal), and *logos* (knowledge), cryptozoology is the "study of hidden animals," or creatures from legends, folklore, or sightings that are not recognized by mainstream science. Originating from the 1950s, the term is generally attributed to Ivan T. Sanderson, a Scottish explorer and author. Cryptid is the term for hidden animals such as the ape-like Bigfoot, long-necked Loch Ness Monster, and blood-sucking chupacabra.

Loren Coleman, widely regarded as the top contemporary cryptozoologist in the world, established the International Cryptozoology Museum in 2003. Located in Portland, Maine, it houses approximately two thousand pieces—from molds of Bigfoot's footprints to movie paraphernalia and taxidermy "specimens" of hoax creatures such as the jackelope. Coleman never takes anything at face value, however, and evaluates all evidence with a critical eye. "I analyze the people involved in sightings," he told the *Boston Globe*. "It's all part of the investigation." But referring to the famous home movie of Bigfoot from 1967, Coleman has doubts that it was a man in a costume because of the way its fur moved on its body. "It's not enough to say Bigfoot exists, but it's enough for us to remain open-minded," he concludes.

On the other hand, some commentators allege that cryptozoology is doomed to the status of pseudoscience, plagued by unscientific methods, insufficient proof, and impossible claims. "The lack of genuine physical and photographic evidence of cryptids constrain cryptozoologists to launch expeditions on the sole basis of so-called reliable eyewitness accounts, leaving them at the mercy of the undeniable constructive nature of perception and memory," insists Elise Schembri, a student at the University of Guelph in Canada. Furthermore, skeptics argue that cryptozoologists do not make major contributions to the discovery of living things. "They are continually looking for long-lost animals without success, but missing the real ones tripped over by undergrads tromping the bushes gathering mundane data on bird droppings," complains Dave Bailey of the Association for Science and Reason. In the following chapter, authors debate the legitimacy of paranormal research, practices, and abilities.

> *"By picking up images and feelings that the untrained mind cannot, I can provide clues, information, and perhaps a new angle to an unsolved crime."*

Psychic Detectives Aid Police Investigations

Noreen Renier

In the following viewpoint, a psychic detective contends that psychic abilities can be a helpful tool in police investigations. Using objects from crime scenes and physical evidence, the author says that she can receive images of a murder and experience the pain and emotions of victims. Still, psychic detectives do not solve crimes, she continues, instead they offer investigators useful information. In addition, she does not claim to have 100 percent accuracy in her interpretations or to be equally effective in every case. Noreen Renier is the author of A Mind for Murder: The Real-Life Files of a Psychic Investigator.

As you read, consider the following questions:

1. What examples from her career history does Renier offer to describe her credibility as a psychic detective?

2. According to Renier, why are law enforcement officials initially skeptical of her psychic abilities?

3. When should a psychic be called into an investigation, in Renier's view?

I have had my throat slit. I have been shot, knifed, stabbed, raped, drowned, and strangled. I have been inside the last moments of many murder victims. I feel their pain, I speak their words, I live their deaths. I see the faces of their murderers, and sometimes I become them. I don't like to get killed more than two or three times a week—it's just too exhausting.

During my career as a psychic detective I have held the bloody earrings, watches, shirts, and shoes of murder victims. I have received the images and feelings that somehow reside in a piece of skull, a vial of blood, a few hairs, the murder weapon. Just as a dog picks up a scent trail that we humans can't detect, my mind taps into the turbulent energy left behind by a moment of explosive violence and I relive the brutal event.

Call it a hunch, a gut feeling, intuition. How do I do it? You tell me. You've been using your logical, rational mind for many years. Explain it to me: How do you use your mind? How did you learn math? How does your memory work? You can't explain it and neither can I. But you can use your mind, and I can use mine.

Psychic Abilities Are Part of Normal Life

I've had quite a ride. Almost twenty-five years ago, on a sunny morning in the midst of an ordinary life as a working single mom, an unconventional career chose me. Since then, I've never looked back. Establishing my credibility in a field that fights for credibility has been daunting, but I have been rewarded in countless ways. In 1981, when I first lectured at the FBI Academy in Quantico, Virginia, my work with the police was considered controversial. Now, I'm a well-known psychic detective who has worked on more than four hundred unsolved homicides, missing persons, and rape cases with city, county, and state law enforcement agencies in thirty-eight states and six foreign countries. My work has been featured in the newspapers, on television, and even in a textbook for homicide detectives.

Like everyone else, I once thought that anyone who had psychic abilities was either a charlatan or a fraud. And just like you, I know that not everyone who calls themselves a psychic really is one. But even though there's no way I can prove to you I'm a psychic, I don't mind being challenged. In 1986, I even took a skeptic to court for calling me a fraud—and won.

I enjoy my work, but it's certainly not the life I would have consciously chosen. Most of all, I want you to understand that psychic abilities are another part of a normal life. They involve no fear, no evil. This ability—the opening of our own minds—is a gift that we can develop for good and use as a wonderful and amazing tool.

Over the years, I have encountered a great deal of fear and ignorance concerning my ability and psychics in general. However, I have discovered one very important thing: If you believe in yourself and in your own efforts, nothing can stand in your way.

How Psychic Connections Help Law Enforcement

I believe that educating people about psychic phenomena is the best way to help people spot charlatans, and the best way to help them open their own minds to new possibilities. It will probably not surprise you to learn that most law enforcement officials are skeptical of my psychic ability the first time we work together. Why shouldn't they be? After all, they are trained to work with facts they can see, touch, and prove. It follows, then, that most of them have not received any training about the best way to work with a psychic on a case. That's why I give the following information to every law enforcement officer I work with before we begin a case.

Why Police Can't Publicize the Use of Psychics and Mediums

- Police are drilled in scientific procedures and forensic science. The culture is very skeptical.

- The police want to appear able to do their job properly without help.

- Government officials don't want to risk being criticized by the media and members of the public about police using psychics and mediums.

- If it became public the police use psychics they would have hundreds of amateur psychics contacting them and wasting their time.

- Suspects in murder cases could get a friend posing as a psychic to contact the police to give them false information.

- Some psychics have been threatened and attacked because their involvement with police was made public. If police find a gifted psychic they want to protect them so they can continue to use them.

Victor Zammit, A Lawyer Presents the Case for the Afterlife, *2006.*
www.victorzammit.com.

Let me state early that I do not solve crimes . . . the police do. I am merely an aid or an investigative tool for the police. By picking up images and feelings that the untrained mind cannot, I can provide clues, information, and perhaps a new angle to an unsolved crime.

The first time a law enforcement officer or agency uses my psychic ability as an investigative tool, it is important to understand a few simple techniques. The following information will help you enhance my psychic abilities during our session and, I hope, bring an unsolved crime to a successful conclusion.

How to Use a Psychic in an Investigation

1. A psychic should be called into an investigation as a last resort, when traditional methods for solving a crime have been exhausted.

2. I prefer not to know any details or personal background of the victim or the crime other than the first name of the victim and the type of crime. The less you tell me, the more I will be able to tell you.

3. I use psychometry, which involves touching an object that the victim wore or the suspect left behind.

4. It is important to start slowly. Initially, I try to see psychically what the victim looked like, or to recreate the scene of the crime. I do this for two reasons: to make sure I am "tuning" in to the case and to give the officer/agent confidence in me as a psychic. If this is successful we can continue with the case.

5. Questions. How you question me will determine the quality of information I receive psychically. *Be prepared.* Know in advance what your objectives are. Think of a profile you want me to fill in, information that will help you to identify and/or locate a suspect or body.

6. The way the questions are phrased is extremely important. An incorrect way to question is: "Where does he (suspect) live?" "Did he (suspect) do it?" A productive way to question is: "Stand in front of the house (body) and walk toward it. What do you see? Look to the right, to the left. Fly above it, what do you see?"

7. Leading questions are not productive. Such questions include: "Is his hair black?" "Was he driving a blue Ford?"

Instead, let me describe him/her to you, as well as any other pertinent information. Questions should have direction and not merely need a "yes" or "no" answer. It is very helpful to give me feedback when you know I have accurately described something or someone. The logical mind can analyze, but the psychic mind just receives information. The feedback keeps my confidence up and the images flowing. "Yes, we understand," is sufficient.

8. Try not to analyze the data that I give you immediately. Think of this part of the session as "fact gathering." Get as much information as you can. Later, you can analyze the information you have received and separate the wheat from the chaff.

9. During the session, I will use all five of my senses to some degree. Ask questions that will make use of these senses. Example: "Is there a special sound near his house (body), a different odor?"

10. My psychic memory is very short. Therefore, it is important that our session be taped. My answers can then be replayed repeatedly or transcribed in order to detect any information that didn't seem important or pertinent earlier.

I do not claim to be 100 percent accurate in my interpretations. Nor do I claim to be able to work on all cases with an equal degree of effectiveness.

Skepticism and Negativism Hamper Psychic Investigators

I do not mind skepticism. However, continued skepticism and negativism hamper my work and concentration. Retired New York Detective Sergeant Vernon Gerberth, writing about my psychic abilities in his textbook *Practical Homicide Investigations*, states:

Practically speaking, if an officer feels that he or she cannot accept or work with the psychic, then this officer should not get involved in this segment of the investigation. Instead, someone who may be skeptical, but is able to put aside this personal prejudice, should be assigned to work with the psychics.

"Other than anecdotal accounts, there are no documented discoveries of missing persons by psychics."

Psychic Detectives Do Not Aid Police Investigations

Peter M. Nardi

In the following viewpoint, a sociologist argues that consultations from psychic detectives do not solve or aid criminal investigations. He declares that psychics have a consistent record of providing false leads. The author says a study revealed that the claims of three psychic detectives were no more accurate than non-psychics in providing information. He concludes that skepticism is necessary to distinguish common-sense observations from actual breaks in cases. Peter M. Nardi is professor emeritus of sociology at Pitzer College in California.

As you read, consider the following questions:

1. What does Nardi believe is "scary" about the percentage of police departments that hired psychics?
2. According to the author, how did the prediction of a successful psychic differ from the reality of the case?

3. As told by Nardi, what did Richard Kocsis conclude about the performance of psychics against others working in investigations?

The afternoon of June 7 [2011], the *New York Times* sent out a news alert: "Up to 30 Dismembered Bodies Found Near Houston, Reuters Reports." CNN also reported that the home near Houston involved "at least 20 bodies, including those of children."

The Liberty County Sheriff's Office obtained a search warrant for the house in Hardin, Texas, and despite some conflicting information related to blood found on a door and strange odors, Texas Rangers were unable to locate any bodies or graves on the site. While all this makes fine fodder for castigating reputable news organization like the *Times*, Reuters and CNN for being too fast on the trigger, Skeptic's Café is interested in another aspect: Houston TV station KPRC reported the investigation all began with a phone call from a psychic.

Yes, a psychic. I knew you were thinking this.

Psychic detectives often show up in stories about missing children, unsolved murders and cold-case crimes. Many people believe that police departments and detectives hire psychics for assistance, but one study found that two-thirds of the 50 largest U.S. police departments have never consulted a psychic to help them out in an unsolved crime. What's a bit scary is that 35 percent did, although many times it is at the request of a family member, and their work typically interfered with the search.

The Failures of Psychic Detectives

How effective are these psychics, and can any of them be good enough to claim noted debunker James Randi's million-dollar offer by showing "under proper observing conditions, evidence of any paranormal, supernatural, or occult power or event"?

Take the story of Portland, Ore., clairvoyant Laurie McQuary. A creative sting was set up by the *Inside Edition* TV show in

March. A producer posing as a distraught brother in search of his missing sister hired McQuary for $400. She looked at the photo of the girl and claimed she had been sexually assaulted and killed, but the case was still solvable. The psychic detective even pointed to a remote location on a map where the body could be found. The next day, McQuary was taped in an interview with an *Inside Edition* correspondent who revealed that the photo was the correspondent as a young girl and not the missing sister of the show's producer. Asked how she could be so wrong, the psychic ended the interview and walked off the set.

A sample of one does not prove the case, but 10 other psychics contacted by the show similarly stated the girl had been murdered. Such errors confirm what the FBI told *Inside Edition*: They were "not aware of any criminal investigation that has been resolved as a direct result of information provided from a psychic."

In another case, dozens of psychics failed to discover a 20-year-old from Tennessee missing since April. Police wasted their time and resources tracking down the false leads. One of the psychics involved even participated in a cable TV show devoted to psychic detectives. (The show was canceled after 22 episodes failed to demonstrate a single case being solved with their supposedly paranormal skills—eerily, the exact same results of a similar show *Down Under*.)

But surely we've heard of some successes by psychic detectives. Consider the case reported in January in the *New York Post*: "A psychic eerily predicted where the victim of a suspected serial killer could be found—nine months before cops dug up the corpse and that of three other young women on a Long Island beach, police sources said."

Claiming to see the body in a grave "overlooking a body of water" with a nearby sign that had the letter "G" in it, did the psychic really "nail it?" Turns out the body was not buried in a grave, any location on Long Island would be near a vaguely described body of water, and no sign was found. And if it had, would the letter "G" be a surprise on Long Island?

The Damage Done by Psychic Detectives

There are many instances of psychics contacting the families of missing children and offering their services—for a fee. The parents are usually so desperate for news that they willingly pay, even if they are skeptical. Even those psychics who do not exploit the bereaved for monetary gain are still hurting instead of helping the situation. Aside from falsely raising the family's hopes, psychic tipsters waste valuable police time and resources following up on the information they provide. Each piece of information is carefully recorded and investigated. Each hour a detective or police officer wastes his or her time chasing dead ends is an hour that could be used trying to find the missing person. And time is especially critical in missing person cases.

Benjamin Radford, "The Stupendous,
Spectacular Failures of Psychic Detectives,"
Proceedings of the Amazing Meeting 4,
James Randi Educational Foundation,
January 26, 2006.

Distinguishing Between Common Sense and Precise Breakthroughs

Skeptical thinking requires that we distinguish between vague, generally applicable common-sense statements and the precise breakthroughs demanded of serious investigations. On closer inspection, other than anecdotal accounts, there are no documented discoveries of missing persons by psychics.

Our critical minds demand some scientific research. Presciently, some studies have looked into psychic detectives. Richard Wiseman, one of the leading researchers on deception and paranormal phenomena, conducted a small study comparing the claims of three psychic detectives to three non-psychic students. They were presented with items that related to actual crimes and "asked to handle each of the objects and speak aloud any ideas, images or thoughts that might be related to these crimes." They were also given statements that were true and false about the already solved crime.

Although the psychic detectives generated more ideas and thoughts than the students, many were obvious and not precise enough to provide helpful information to detectives. And the difference in accuracy between the students and psychics was not statistically significant. Neither group performed better than chance would predict.

Richard Kocsis, a leading Australian forensic psychologist, has extensively studied professional criminal psychological profilers and concludes that properly trained profilers help focus an investigation better than other comparison groups of psychologists, police detectives and psychics. In fact, he demonstrates "little support for the use of psychics in accurately generating the characteristics of an unknown offender." Psychics performed the worst of all; they were unable to provide information beyond what common sense or "the local bartender might be able to surmise."

I don't know about you, but at this point, after hearing about all these psychics falsely claiming success in solving crimes, I can easily predict that it's time for a long discussion with the local bartender. I knew you were thinking this.

"[Mediums] have this innate gift . . . yet most scientists were just dismissing the whole thing outright."

Mediums Communicate with the Dead

Julie Beischel, interviewed by Dean Radin

In the following viewpoint, a parapsychologist interviews a re-searcher about evidence demonstrating that mediums can commu-nicate with the dead. The researcher claims that in blinded experi-ments, mediums consistently gave readings that were significant to sitters—the family member or survivor—and the deceased they wished to contact. Therefore, she insists that mediumship has great therapeutic value to grieving individuals and should be offered along with counseling and accepted as a routine practice. Julie Beischel is co-founder and director of research of the Windbridge Institute for Applied Research in Human Potential. Dean Radin is a parapsychologist and senior scientist at the Institute of Noetic Sciences.

As you read, consider the following questions:

1. In Beischel's words, why did she begin to research mediumship?

2. What is Beischel's view of the benefits of traditional grief counseling?

3. How do mediums have an "altered sense of time," as described by Beischel?

Dean Radin: I want to ask you a question that you likely get a lot. How did a nice young lady with a doctorate in toxicology and pharmacology end up doing mediumship research?

[Julie] Beischel: I do get asked that a lot. It's a long story, but the short version is that when I was in graduate school, my mom committed suicide. I was twenty-four at the time. Science is my religion, and I turned to science to see what it had to say about the afterlife. Although there were some things being done, I found science did not have very many answers.

I had a reading from a medium, and from my personal experience, I recognized that there was clearly something going on there. I have a strong sense of justice, and it angered me to know that there are people in the world who have this innate gift of what they experience as communication from the other side, which they want to use to help people, yet most scientists were just dismissing the whole thing outright, without any information about the reality of it. So I got on my soapbox and began my scientific investigative pursuit.

The Belief in Consciousness After Death

A lot of scientists are interested in these kinds of questions, questions about survival, but they don't take the time and the care to study the data long enough to be able to tweak their prior beliefs. So, as you said, if science is your religion—at least within the Western science tradition—when you're dead, you're dead. The brain is the mind, and that's the end of the story. You must have had a lot of motivation to push through that argument, which is what most college students get, certainly by the time they finish their doctorate. Was there anything other than the mediumship experience that motivated you? What about the literature that you read afterward?

What happens when we die never came up when I studied for my degree in the medical field, so I didn't have any preconceived notions. I was never taught that the brain creates the mind; it didn't take a lot for me to get over that. I was a blank slate. Before my mom died, I didn't even know what a medium was. That first personal experience was moving. You know, people can look at our data and our P values until the end of time, but when they have one reading, it makes all the difference. That's what happened to me. I had this personal experience that demonstrated that something was going on here that required further investigation, and I had no preconceived notions about my investigation.

As a biologist you have probably been around lots of studies involving mice and other animals. Given your perspective now, do you imagine that when the mice are euthanized, after doing whatever experiment they've done, that they continue on to mouse heaven somewhere? Are there little departed mice out there?

I hope so. I think the example most people can relate to is with their pets or companion animals. I know my dog has consciousness; I have no doubt about that. The question is how far back can we go in the evolutionary tree to where consciousness stops. Do amoeba have consciousness? These are questions we don't have answers to now. Animal consciousness is a topic we're interested in at Windbridge [Institute for Applied Research in Human Potential]. Mark Boccuzzi, my husband and cofounder of Windbridge, did a presentation with me at the Florida Sciences Consciousness Conference on a study we did with our dog and a random event generator. . . .

How Mediumship Experiments Work

I wonder if this is relevant to the connection between a person who is living and a departed loved one. I can see that there might be a link, but then how does the medium come into play? How does a medium make that link?

When we do our quintuple-blind experiments, there are five levels of blinding. The medium and I are on the telephone, and all we have is the first name of the deceased person—we're both blinded. I give the medium the first name—let's say, "Jack"—and then I ask a number of specific questions about Jack. People wonder how the medium finds Jack. It's not up to the medium; Jack finds the medium. Most mediums will experience communication before the reading even starts. So before I even call, Jack is already there trying to get through to the medium, who is literally a channel. Mediums just report what shows up.

How does Jack know that Jack is going to be the person you want to contact? What is your guess?

I think that once you are not bodily bound, you have access to nonlocal information. Jack knows what medium's name is in my planner next to his name, and he is able to find her.

I recently started a blog. I post behind-the-scenes things that don't end up in journal articles but that are interesting and perhaps evidential. Recently we did a lot of readings to test a number of new mediums. We were collecting data for a study. My planner is full of deceased people's names and mediums' names, and it turned out that there were two deceased people with the same first name—we use the first name to protect the privacy of the deceased. So, two deceased people named Sally were supposed to be read on the same day, and I just held my planner up to the universe as if to say *you guys are going to have to figure this out because I don't know who goes with whom.* Well, the first medium became ill and couldn't do the reading. We rescheduled, and then the other Sally got her own day. It all worked out, oddly enough. There was no confusion because only one Sally got read on a given day. So, they have a way to work it out: there must be some sort of awesome receptionist on the other side, or I don't know—but someone is organizing something over there.

Let's back up a second so that you can describe not the quintuple blindness, but a simple version of at least a double-blind medium-ship experiment.

A single-blind mediumship reading is where the medium is blinded to any information about the deceased person, but the experimenter knows who the deceased person is or who the sitter is—that sort of information. Once you also blind the experimenter, the experiment becomes double-blinded. In those cases, for example, I get on at a scheduled time and call the medium with a first name of a deceased person. (This requires more people being involved—someone who gives me the name but is blind to other parts of the study.) So, the medium and I only have the first name of the deceased person. I call and say, "The person's name is Jack," and then we ask four questions about Jack when he was alive. We ask for a description of his physical appearance, his personality, his hobbies or activities or how he spent his time, and the cause of death. If you have that information about any given person, you can pretty much determine if it's the person you're looking to hear from. Once that's established, we ask, "Does Jack have any comments, questions, requests or messages for the sitter?" After all, we've asked Jack to jump through all our science hoops, so the least he should be able to do is provide information for the living person who is interested in hearing from him. We call this person "the sitter."

Mediumship Experiments Offer Significant Results

I presume you record these sessions.

Yes, we audio record. The definitions of blinding do get complicated because you could also think of the sitter as blinded. It's just the medium and me on the phone, so the sitter doesn't hear the reading. The living person who wants to hear from Jack doesn't hear the reading. The medium and I do that whole process a second time on a different day with a different deceased person—let's say, "Bob." We ask the same questions about Bob, and that session is also audio-recorded.

Then I take those recordings and turn them into itemized lists. Each numbered item is a single piece of information: he had brown hair, blue eyes, whatever the different pieces of information about the deceased are. Those two lists are then emailed to the two sitters, the people who lost Jack and Bob, but they don't know which one is which. The readings have been blinded. Then they score each reading as to how it applies to their deceased person and pick which one they think belongs to them. We compare the scores a person gave his or her own reading to the scores he or she gave the other person's reading. We look at that difference.

And what do the results of such experiments show?

They're pretty strongly significant. In a study we published some years ago, 13 out of 16 people were able to choose their own reading from the two. We're currently replicating that published study with a much larger one.

How important is it that the medium is a medium? In other words, if there were something like a control medium, someone who didn't profess any ability to be able to do this, would the control get chance results on that?

I would assume so, yes. What we see is that when someone scores someone else's reading, they're usually about 20 to 25 percent correct. So about a quarter of the information that a medium provides might relate to someone else. That's not a criticism of mediums or mediumship. It just shows how similar we are as people and that there are going to be things that are true for everybody.

Mediumship Is "Not So Miraculous"

One of the things I think is unique about Windbridge is the large number of mediums that have passed through a variety of hoops to make sure that they are actually as good as they think they are. Would you describe this process of forming what you call the "research medium"?

We have an eight-step process. First, I should point out that we're not looking for any new mediums. We have a bunch going through the eight steps at this time—currently the six mediums on our website have passed all eight steps. I won't go through them all now; there are a lot of tests, interviews, and blinded readings. Once a person passes step five, the blinded reading part, he or she goes on to be trained. We've found that about 25 percent of people who think they're good enough to pass our stringent testing do no better than chance.

Does that mean that 75 percent actually do pass?

Yeah, that is a little surprising, but the screening is so daunting that only people who are really confident they can do it even attempt it. Also, a Windbridge certified research medium agrees to volunteer four hours per month for this research, so only people really interested in the scientific pursuit of this investigation and willing to dedicate part of their life to it even attempt our certification process.

I understand that it's a highly select group. Still, for 75 percent of the applicants to have a very special talent like that is pretty impressive.

I think that goes to show that it's not so miraculous. A lot of people can do it, and a lot of people can do it very well. I've heard a number of mediums say that they aren't special, and they don't like to be called that. It rubs them the wrong way when they hear other mediums—on TV or whatever—talk about how special they are and how unique this is. A lot of mediums will say their job is to put themselves out of business, because if one human brain can do this, then anybody can. I think it's probably closer to how in parapsychology the word *virtuoso* is often used for people who are just born with this ability and can do it right off. Some people can practice and practice but never be as good as a virtuoso. There are probably tips, but a lot of mediums say you just have to be open. You have to learn to let go of all the cognitive blocks you and others have put on yourself that say this isn't possible and can't be done by you. . . .

The Therapeutic Benefits of Mediumship

Given that you've spent the last seven years or so doing mediumship research and have published a number of papers, where do you see this line of research going in five to ten years? For example, would it be possible that the cumulative data would actually start to persuade people who previously wouldn't have given you the time of day? Would you have enough data to persuade them that at minimum something really interesting is going on and that at maximum there really is survival?

Well, we are the Windbridge Institute for Applied Research, so we want to know how this can benefit humanity and best serve all living things. I think, though, that we could gather data to no end, and it still wouldn't convince some people. I've had P values [statistically significant results] and peer-reviewed journal articles, and still people say, "Oh no, it's just a fluke." There is a cognitive block; I'm not going to waste my time banging my head against the wall to convince people who refuse to see that something is going on here. So we've gone down another path: what can we do with this, and how can this help?

We recently presented some pilot data about the potential therapeutic benefits of a mediumship reading. We propose that a mediumship reading would be a great treatment option for grief. There's a lot of evidence that spontaneous or even induced after-death communication has a great effect on personal grief. A recent meta-analysis performed at the University of Memphis on 64 studies demonstrated this. Traditional grief counseling wasn't benefiting the patients any better than the passage of time and the resources of support a person already had. An effective grief therapy is not currently out there. People who have had a mediumship meeting report some miraculous, instantaneous changes. I think that a lot of grief counselors would agree that to get past grief you have to redefine your relationship with the deceased. A mediumship reading allows you to do that. We foresee a future where someone can have a mediumship reading and take the information the medium provided to a counselor to integrate that information.

Another arm of our research is studying the mediums' experiences. We've demonstrated that they have an altered sense of time—mediums are not really present for the reading as it takes place. I describe this as when you're on the phone with someone who is giving you a phone number and you're saying it out loud to a person in the room who is writing it down. As soon as you're done, you don't know what that phone number was because you were just repeating it as the other person was saying it to you. That's what mediums do; they're not in a space that allows them to be a counselor—and they shouldn't have to be.

Mediums and grief counselors together could make a difference in people's lives. Grief is really at the root of so many pathologies, addiction and all kinds of things. I think there is a real need for this. Recently, I told [pioneering psi researcher] Charlie Tart that I foresee a future where an insurance company will pay for a mediumship reading, and Charlie laughed. He said

I had big dreams. But I don't think that this is so crazy. It wasn't that long ago that insurance companies wouldn't pay for acupuncture, and now a lot of them do. I think that this is the future and that we just need to demonstrate the efficacy so they cave to public pressure. People are spending billions of dollars anyway; let's certify mediums so people can go to a reputable one.

"*Mediums cannot show they do
anything more than cold reading nor
that what the TV audience sees is just
selectively edited to show 'hits' and
ignore the 'misses.'*"

The *Medium* Is Not
the Messenger

James Randi

*In the following viewpoint, James Randi asserts that mediums do
not have the ability to contact the dead. Randi explains how mediums use a tactic called "cold reading" to make vague observations
seem personal. This is particularly troubling, he says, because the
practice preys on people who are at their most vulnerable. James
Randi is a retired professional stage magician and the founder of
the James Randi Educational Foundation.*

As you read, consider the following questions:

1. As described by Randi, what is the Forer effect?
2. According to Randi, what do psychologists say about the
   effect of mediums on people who are grieving the loss of
   loved ones?
3. Why was TLC given a Pigasus Award?

Hardly does one talking-to-the-dead practitioner fade from view than another pops up, to the delight of the naifs who desperately need assurance that no one ever really dies but somehow instead just floats off to heaven, Valhalla, paradise or whatever Cloud Nine they fancy—to, um, "live" forever.

John Edward is now holding court in Las Vegas, and James Van Praagh still coos to his eagerly paying public in hotel auditoriums, but the newest (and far more attractive) dead-talker is the *Long Island Medium*, featured on the Learning Channel. She's Theresa Caputo, a chatty blonde with impressive layers of eyeliner and lip gloss who does the old dependable "cold reading" act, and has rung their bell . . .

The Learning Channel has, sadly, recognized—along with so many other such outlets—that pseudo-science attracts viewers. They've reached their own private nirvana with Ms. Caputo.

Caputo does what's known in my trade as "cold reading." The very best practitioners can pick up enough information in what seems like innocent, idle conversation to convince you that they know very specific things about you. The scientific phenomenon is called the Forer effect—giving credence to vague observations that seem personal.

It's called the Barnum effect, after that famous showman credited with coining the phrase: "There's a sucker born every minute."

That technique consists of simply tossing out initials, names and situations to the subject, asking casual questions while guessing, and a handful of other manipulative psychological techniques to appear to be demonstrating psychic powers.

"Is there an anniversary coming up?" "A birthday or something?" "He/she just said to me . . ." "He's proud of you" and the ever-popular "Do you understand?"—to which the answer is always a nod of assent. What else is a beguiled believer to do when told: "She's happy in Heaven?"

All of those inquiries come from Caputo, I should add.

Why do these pseudo-psychic spectacles bother those of us at the James Randi Educational Foundation? First, and foremost:

"We'll start by typing in—IS THERE ANYBODY THERE—then click SEARCH," cartoon by Gordon Gurvan. www.CartoonStock.com.

They are not true. TV psychics do not talk to the dead (nor do the dead talk back to them!). Mediums cannot show they do anything more than cold reading nor that what the TV audience sees is just selectively edited to show "hits" and ignore the "misses."

But much more importantly to us, such performances seem to prey on people at their most vulnerable moments—those who have suffered the loss of loved ones—and these mediums use such grief to make a buck. Psychologists tell us this keeps the grieving stuck in their grief, rather than going through the natural stages of acceptance that are healthy.

It is for this reason that JREF just last week gave Caputo the prized Pigasus Award in the performer category for 2012. (We named the awards after both the mythical flying horse Pegasus of Greek mythology and the highly improbable flying pig of popular cliché.) The official Pigasus Awards announcement is below.

For many years now, we have bestowed the Pigasus Award as an annual recognition of the most egregious examples of flim-flammery—the most deserving charlatans, swindlers, psychics, pseudoscientists and faith healers, along with their corporate enablers—and TLC also won the Pigasus this year in the media category, for its work promoting Caputo and her harmful act to such wide audiences.

Caputo is just one more of the myriad faux seers who have stepped into the TV spotlight for their turn, and though her exuberant shtick rather outdoes the others, she'll do her number along with Sylvia Browne, Van Praagh, John Edward and "Psychic Sally" until someone with a newer novelty elbows her offstage.

> *"Studies in the paranormal should progress along with normal science, follow normal scientific trends and be recognized by the mainstream scientific community."*

The Study of Paranormal Phenomena Is Legitimate Science

Jack Porter

In the following viewpoint, a paranormal investigator states that the study of paranormal phenomena has scientific validity. He contends that true paranormal investigators use the standard of objectivity in mainstream science and approach investigations as skeptics, first searching for natural or logical explanations. In fact, he states that they work to eliminate fraud and deception from the field, and paranormal research has yielded information useful to the scientific community. Jack Porter is co-founder of the Erie County Paranormal Association in Buffalo, New York.

As you read, consider the following questions:

1. How does the author respond to the presence of "thrill-seekers" in the paranormal field?

2. How has parapsychology contributed to psychology, as claimed by Porter?

3. According to Porter, why is the evidence paranormal investigators produced for Bigfoot legitimate?

With the increase in weekly television series that center themselves on paranormal investigations, the debate over whether or not investigations into the paranormal have any scientific merit is ever popular. With this, it is important to point out that mainstream science should recognize evidence collected in paranormal investigations.

As any scientist knows, there are two main types of evidence and a good paranormal investigator knows the same. It is necessary that the evidence collected be objective (dependent upon external, unbiased measurement equally obtainable by all) and not subjective (dependent upon an observer's limited perception) in order to be considered legitimate. With this standard being utilized in mainstream science as well as paranormal investigations, there should be no argument as to whether or not the appropriate type of evidence was collected.

Another concept that mainstream science needs to understand is that a true paranormal investigator goes into an investigation as a skeptic. In the book, *The Skeptic's Guide to the Paranormal*, the author [Lynn Kelly] gives a number of natural explanations for what may be causing paranormal activity in a haunting case. Some of the explanations she gives are: temperature changes, central heating, moisture in wood, plumbing problems in the location and swamp gas. However, as stated before, when an investigator enters into an investigation, the first thing they attempt to do is find a natural explanation for the occurrence. Once all natural explanations have failed (also called debunking) then and only then is the situation considered paranormal. Or as [investigator] Joshua Warren puts it:

Just because you're studying extraordinary activity, that doesn't mean you should abandon ordinary logic. Always remember the scientific principle known as Occam's Razor: In order to define a fact, assume as little as possible. The simplest explanation for a phenomenon is usually the correct one, and the less you take for granted, the more solid your conclusion will be.

Not assuming anything and keeping the explanation simple will only lend credibility to the investigation and evidence collected.

Throughout history there have been a number of individuals who have been personally persecuted (or their family members) due to their beliefs that the science of the time was incorrect. For instance, [scientist and astronomer] Johannes Kepler's mother was put on trial and tortured for witch craft due to Kepler's belief that the geocentric astronomy (seven planets moved around the earth) taught at the time was not accurate. If not for his continual effort, research, evidence collection and presentation, it is hard to say how much longer it would have been before the "scientists" of the time would have accepted the fact that not everything in the universe revolves around the earth.

Planetary alignment has not been the only situation where science has been proven to be inaccurate. There was once a time when natural occurrences such as lightning, lunar or solar eclipses, earthquakes and weather patterns were considered paranormal or an act of the gods. Through proper investigations and collection of evidence, it has been shown that the above listed occurrences are a natural part of our environment. With this in mind, it is important for the scientific community to remember what author and scientist Carl Sagan has been quoted as saying, "absence of evidence is not evidence of absence".

Paranormal Investigators Are Trained and Educated in the Field

It is true that some investigators into the paranormal are thrill-seekers that truly have no idea how to conduct a proper investigation and even less of an idea of how to collect evidence or even what evidence to collect. However, there are paranormal investigators whose livelihood depends on paranormal activities, and they have been specifically trained and educated in the field, they are known as parapsychologists. The field of parapsychology is full of legitimate trained scientists and investigators and they tend to centralize their work around the unknown portions of the mind as well as the investigation of hauntings of ghosts.

When talking about parapsychologists studying the human mind, it does not mean they are looking into the normal five senses of taste, touch, hear, smell and see. They are looking more into what some call the sixth sense—extrasensory perception or E.S.P. for short. The main reason parapsychologists have crossed over into such areas as "ghost hunting", is because some believe that the two are indirectly connected.

Parapsychologists have had a significant impact on mainstream science, especially in the area of psychology. Early parapsychologists or members of the Society of Psychical Research as referred to prior to parapsychology's existence, contributed greatly to the development of ideas concerning psychological studies of the subconscious mind and dissociation.

Another area parapsychologists have taken a great role, one that may be of interest to mainstream science because theoretically parapsychologists are attempting to put themselves out of work, is that of the study of fraud and self-deception. In other words, parapsychologists are investigating events such as mediumship, apparitions, poltergeist activities, metal bending and reincarnation to uncover fraudulent reports. Their main reason for doing this is to weed out the fraudulent cases, and those with the potential to be legitimate are investigated and the evidence is gathered and analyzed.

Given the areas that are being researched by paranormal investigators, and the fact that at this point in time there are no explanations to the events, it should not be assumed that just because an individual does not have a doctorate or master's degree in parapsychology or some other type of science, that they should not be considered a legitimate source of information from either field or laboratory investigations.

There Is a Legitimate Need for Paranormal Research

Paranormal investigations in the laboratory have provided some very useful information to the scientific community. This information, however, as not proven anything as of yet, but it has lead to some very interesting theories. It is important to remember that the Big Bang is a theory, but that is still considered science. One theory within the paranormal investigations community is that everything, to include living organisms, has a very subtle magnetic field. On their way to proving this theory, researchers at the University of Nijmegen in the Netherlands have made small living creatures such as frogs and spiders levitate. This has been accomplished by placing the creature into a chamber that is only inches in diameter, and exposing the chamber to an extremely powerful magnet from beneath. The result is the creature begins to levitate. This has been explained as being similar to placing the northern polarity of two magnets together; they repel each other.

Another method that is being utilized to prove the theory that everything has a magnetic field is with the use of special photography called Kirlian photography. Investigators have been able to photograph this potential magnetic field around items to include the human body. It has also been shown that the strength of the field is stronger in some people than others. If the scientific community would acknowledge these findings, the information could be expanded upon and quite possibly a new way to detect illness or injury could be developed. It could also be deduced that if this theory is correct and a magnetic energy field does exists around the human body, wouldn't Albert Einstein's theory that energy cannot be created or destroyed support the belief that when we physically die, the energy remains behind?

Academic Interest in the Paranormal Has Increased

Parapsychologists, who have historically investigated hauntings with rigorous academic protocols, lament the layman's approach. Yet, more academically oriented people are interested in the field than ever, despite a lack of institutional support. This includes quantum physicists, psychologists, and others who may take some aspects of this research to universities for real examination. There is hope that as more evidence is collected, there will be a stronger argument for funded research. Numerous hurdles exist before this can become a reality. The biggest challenge is how to fit paranormal events into scientific methodology. At the grassroots level, there is spectacular technological innovation and sincere dialogue regarding philosophy and methodology of the paranormal.

Deonna Kelli Sayed, America's
Fascination with Ghosts and Hauntings,
Spooks and Spirits. *Woodbury, MN: Llewellyn
Publications, 2011.*

The need for paranormal research is not only legitimate, but absolute. Taking into considerations the definition of paranormal; para meaning "beyond" thus paranormal meaning any events beyond the realm of normal occurrence or belief, all science would be a form of paranormal research. Science is in itself a quest to learn, a quest to know the unknown. As scientists, you understand that just because a certain situation or event cannot be recreated in a laboratory, it does not mean it does not exist or cannot occur, again the Big Bang Theory. However, when it comes to paranormal activities, that is exactly how some organizations react. They believe if they cannot recreate an apparition per se, then it must be a hallucination or a hoax.

It is understandable that some feel this way due to the fact that the majority of paranormal cases that have made it into mainstream media have been identified as a hoax. One such case is that of the "Amityville Horror". This case obtained worldwide notoriety in the form of books, movies and sequels to the original movie. Unfortunately for the community of paranormal investigators, it has been confirmed as a hoax. Situations like this are what give those who are serious about investigating the paranormal a bad name and make it that much harder for their evidence or theories to be accepted.

Luckily for scientists, there has never been a situation like this. That is not actually true; in 1912 a creature was found in a gravel pit in Sussex England that was claimed to be the missing link. It took scientists 40 years to figure out that the corpse that was found was actually man made by combining a humanlike brain case and an ape's jaw. With this hoax in mind, should anthropology or Darwinism be written off as to not having any scientific merit due to the acts of one individual attempting to gain media attention? Of course not, because the whole cannot be judged by the actions of a few. Especially considering the legitimate evidence that has been presented by anthropologists that have helped us as a species determine where we have come from.

Cryptozoology Acknowledges the Paranormal

The hunt for the missing link or other such creatures is not limited to anthropologists, zoologists or cryptozoologists. Paranormal investigators are also on the hunt for what some believe is the missing link, Bigfoot.

The hunt for evidence of the existence of Bigfoot has also gone unnoticed by mainstream science with the exception of one area, cryptozoology. This is a step in the right direction with regards to mainstream science and paranormal investigators working together. With the two different realms of investigators working together, some very interesting evidence has been brought to light that surely suggest that there may be some merit to the claims of many paranormal investigators.

One piece of evidence collected by paranormal investigators that has been acknowledged by cryptozoologists is that of plaster casts that have shown dermal ridges. This is an extremely important discovery and piece of evidence bringing paranormal investigators one step closer in proving the existence of Bigfoot. The reason being is because all humans and prime apes have dermal ridges, a.k.a. fingerprints. Plaster casts from around the world have been examined by experts and it has shown that, yes, some are a fake, but for the most part, these are legitimate casts of some type of creature.

Another piece of evidence that has been analyzed time and time again by paranormal investigators and cryptozoologists is Roger Patterson's 1967 film of Bigfoot walking across an open area. Under close examination many cryptozoologists claim to be able to actually see different muscle groups in the shoulder and back of the creature. This is a very significant statement due to the fact that many in mainstream science believe it is nothing more than a man in a suit. If muscle groups can be determined from the film, how is it possible that this creature is a man in a suit?

If cryptozoologists have no problem working with paranormal investigators in finding the ultimate truth behind the Bigfoot phenomena, then why are there not more mainstream scientists coming forward in other areas? How long would the mystery of the Loch Ness Monster, or Lake Champlain's counterpart, Champ, go on if marine biologists gave the eyewitness testimony and photographs currently on record proper credit?

Paranormal Phenomena Are Studied in Good Faith

Paranormal investigations have been occurring throughout history in one way or another. In some cases, these investigations or studies of the situation were made and proved fraud and deception, but in many cases, paranormal phenomena have been studied in good faith in an effort to verify their authenticity and discover the source of the phenomena. Believers in the paranormal consider study of the paranormal to be scientifically valid, but the few scientists who conduct research in the paranormal often do so without "official" support. Some of the scientists that believe in either the truth or possibility of the paranormal do not believe it is a scientific priority, but an extremely minor effect and not worthy of "official" support. At most then, the support of the scientific community has been minimal, yet if the paranormal is scientific in that paranormal phenomena are reducible and explainable in logical terms, then studies in the paranormal should progress along with normal science, follow normal scientific trends and be recognized by the mainstream scientific community.

"Dressing up and acting all sciencey-like is a tactic used by . . . cryptozoologists, ghost hunters, and UFOlogists, among others."

The Study of Paranormal Phenomena Is Not Legitimate Science

Sharon Hill

In the following viewpoint, a skeptic expresses doubts about the scientific legitimacy of paranormal studies. The author asserts that many paranormal research groups co-opt aspects of science to gain credibility. Particularly, she scrutinizes groups touting the scientific method, claiming that the investigators' procedures were subjective or only sounded scientific. However, paranormal research groups continue to exaggerate the seriousness and importance of their work to the public, which must be challenged, she argues. Sharon Hill is the founder of Doubtful News, *a blog on skepticism.*

As you read, consider the following questions:

1. What frequently happens under the label of "science," according to the author?

2. As stated by Hill, what did the paranormal research groups she contacted mean by using the scientific method?

3. What two things does the author observe about "sciencey-sounding" groups?

S cience.

It is a bit hard to define what that is. Meanings change through time. If you are one who values science as the most reliable way to understand the world, you likely have a much stronger definition of the term than someone who values it less. Science is all these things: a process, a way of looking at a topic, a community, an infrastructure, a career, a set of results, an authority, and more. We can use the word in many ways. That means it can be abused in many ways as well.

[Science studies professor] Daniel Patrick Thurs's aptly named book *Science Talk* is an interesting walk through how we have historically talked about science. He takes us through the terms and rhetoric that the public and purveyors of sciences used through the development of the scientific age and demonstrates how meanings are constructed based on the needs we have at any time.

Popular ideas about science have evolved significantly since the word came to be. At first, it just meant *a body of reliable and systematized knowledge.* That really general way of referring to "a science" was in use until the early 1800s. When "scientist" became an actual profession—where certain training was expected, amateurs were pushed out, and a unique jargon was developed—*boundaries* formed (and were actively built) around science.

Constructed boundaries enhanced the reputation of science as a distinctive (perhaps "honored") way of knowing about the world and excluded that which wasn't science (conveniently judged by the scientists themselves).

The new and improved version of "science" now encompassed all the activities which, collectively, serve the aim of explaining the natural world and how it works.

As the scientific community organized into an "establishment," an ethos [group of practices] developed. Certain standards of practice were expected of a "scientist," foremost of which was the entrance to the club through higher education.

Scientific discoveries contributed to human societies in (mostly) positive ways; therefore, the prestige of being "scientific" grew. "Scientific" was associated with being "more true" and more reliable. The biggest drawback of this prestige—which was derived from the rigor and professionalism of science—was that the scientific community itself and the capacity to understand how science really worked receded from the grasp of the non-science public. Being a scientist was special because not everyone could do it. Being scientific was a high standard. Science was hard.

Oversimplifying the Scientific Method

Science progresses on a path quite different from what the public sees. Regular surveys about the public understanding of science tell us that the non-scientist doesn't comprehend well the importance of critical concepts like controlled trials, peer review, skeptical criticism, and the holding of ideas as provisional. It's not a surprise that the public doesn't get how science works; they aren't exposed to it. People form their ideas about science from the input they DO get—mostly from basic education and popular culture.

In order to do science and be scientific, we are told, you must follow the scientific method.

Once upon a time, though, "scientific method" was not part of the common vernacular. When it began to be used, in the mid-19th century, it was synonymous with "thorough" and "careful."

Perhaps your first introduction to science may have been in elementary school, when you were taught the "scientific method" presented as a step-by-step prescription to investigate nature that went something like this: observe and gather facts; derive the question you need answered about those facts; propose an explanation for the facts that answers that question; test that explanation.

Sounds easy enough for anyone to do! But, it's an oversimplification for today's complicated world. There really is no foolproof, formulaic method that one can apply to all subject areas. Even diligently using the above process, one can go off the rails immediately and end up with nonsense.

Right off the mark, we are all noticeably poor observers—we assume many "facts" that have not actually been confirmed. Many trip up constructing the proper question in order to get a precise, meaningful answer. People regularly make utterly untestable hypotheses (e.g., invoke supernatural causes) then bias the evidence collection process to support a favored explanation, run bogus tests to confirm it, package their conclusions in an enticing way, and then sell it to others. Indeed, this happens all the time, often under the label of "science."

Ghost Science Has No Substance

Instead of playing by the established rules, fields of study with premises that have been rejected by mainstream science attempt an end run around the scientific process. Working backwards from conclusions to evidence so they can support their pet ideas, they co-opt the symbols and processes of science. Dressing up and acting all sciencey-like is a tactic used by intelligent design advocates/creationists, cryptozoologists, ghost hunters, and UFOlogists, among others. It's a handy gimmick—one that is frequently effective with the public as laypersons may not notice the missing rigor. That it works so often is a reflection of how shallowly the public understands science.

For example, let's examine the popular paranormal-based hobby of ghost hunting/paranormal investigation.

About half of all paranormal research groups prominently boast that they use a/the "scientific method." (Whether they use the definite or indefinite article, you will see, does not matter at all.) They frequently present themselves this way to clients, public audiences, and the media.

Curious as to what they meant by that, I contacted a number of paranormal research groups that specifically said they used a "scientific method" or "science" in their methodology. I picked several that *really* spread the scienceyness on thick. "Science" was in their name or appeared to be of great importance to them. If they promoted science so strongly, were they, in fact, scientists? Did they have a well-thought-out protocol? Since science is a community activity and you are expected to put your findings out there for others to critique, I expected they would be confident in sharing their work with others and defending their conclusions.

Not so much.

The replies I received, though few, spanned a curious range from haughty self-confidence to realistic admissions of failure.

Paranormal Researchers Can't Defend Their Work

When asked if any of their group members had experience in scientific research outside the paranormal group, a few said "No" outright but several hyped their personal background, equating their ghost investigation activities, computer science experience, or electronics expertise with "scientific training." That's not only odd but disingenuous, stretching even *the most* generic idea of "scientific."

What did they mean by a *scientific method?* As I anticipated from the emphasis on gadgetry on their websites, they defined their methods in terms of objectivity, such as data collection through use of equipment. But, nearly universally, their idea of being scientific was simply to be *methodical* and *systematic.* For one group their idea of doing science was only "in depth research and investigation," harkening back to the original and nonspecific idea of science as the organized study of anything.

Nonetheless, many who claim to be objective use various subjective means of investigation: intuitives (psychics), dowsing, pendulums, and even Ouija boards.

One particular group with the word "sciences" in its name offers classes to the community on *how to investigate using a scientific method*. My respondent replied to the question "What about your methods is scientific?" with the elementary definition: identify problem, form hypothesis, test, and conclude. She also added that they were "creating a model of examined evidence or data then trying out different hypothesis." That sounds sufficiently perspicacious and purposeful, but according to the investigation results from their fancy-worded website they weren't producing anything testable or vaguely coherent enough to be called a "model." Their "facts" were more appropriately labeled "opinions," "feelings," or "stories." Their conclusions were unsupported and biased by their obvious belief in paranormal explanations.

Finally, I queried the host of a local radio show called *Paranormal Science* (You can't get much more sciencey than that!) who proved to be both the most vague and the most direct at the same time. The group leader said, "I think what we are referring to is 'as scientific as possible with the means we have.'" Contrasting this to the use of metaphysical means of investigation (i.e., psychics or occult means), they wish to document "hard" evidence, yet admit they are never in a position to fully control the environment.

I would guess that this is the first time anyone has asked them questions about science as they outright concede, "We by no means are using THE Scientific methods [*sic*]. Just various 'as-scientific' methods or ways of trying to document activity."

I was puzzled. Calling themselves "scientific" where there was admittedly no science going on was dodgy, to say the least. When I had asked if they had science training, I got a resounding "Yes!" but no details. When they started talking about quantum physics and "energy," I figured out they knew enough high-falutin' sciencey talk to be dangerous to the public, who are often too easily impressed by a cheap tuxedo, so to speak.

I saw them as science poseurs who were playing up a manufactured sense of self-importance. They wanted to "take an intelligent look at all this stuff, or at least a common sense approach. LOL."

In a P.S. to my reply, the *Paranormal Science* show host blew the game by conceding, "The 'science' in *Paranormal Science* just refers to the 'workings' behind various topics we will be covering. It has nothing to do with actual science. Just a catch phrase. LOL!"

LOLs indeed. . . .

I observed two things about these sciencey-sounding groups. First, they had little to no idea what modern science is or how to do it. Instead, they were operating on their perceived, old-fashioned idea of what sounded sufficiently sciencey and impressive to them. Second, they were co-opting the memes of science to appear serious and careful. They were perfectly comfortable playing scientists to their clients, the media, and the public, who assumed they were conscientious. But when someone who knew a little more about standards of real science knocked on the door to question them, they shifted their ground. Their methods were not scientific; their work was not science at all.

Counterfeit Science Should Be Challenged

I reached Daniel Thurs, the author of *Science Talk*, via email to ask why he thought these researchers who claim to use science immediately backpedaled from the strong version of the term when I questioned them on it.

The "scientific method," he said, "seems to be one of the most portable parts of science."

It works because it's vague and it sounds prescriptive. Anyone can use it. When one tries to pin down exactly what aspects of science they are practicing and how they achieve each step in a scientific method, the smoky vagueness has to be cleared up.

Are they possibly using the term "scientific method" to suppress debate? "Look! We use the scientific method so we obtain reliable results and are superior to that group who is just out to have fun." If that's a purpose, the usefulness is diminished by my questioning, which sent them scrambling to places where they were obviously uncomfortable (thus causing random outbursts of acronymical laughter).

But it's not funny. These researchers claiming to use the scientific method failed to understand that science is powerful in our society precisely because it is *hard* and not everyone can do it. Instead, they adopted the gimmick of sprinkling "scientific method" and other sciencey-sounding words around because others relate to that and associate that with being more correct or genuine.

It is difficult to talk concisely about the practice of faking science, even though it is so prevalent. The words available to me were just not adequate to express what I was trying to say. I went through books and essays about "stuff" done outside of scientific orthodoxy. It was labeled as pseudoscience. Alternatively, one could be said to be conjuring science, constructing a scientific façade, imitating science, etc. The methods and ideas were described as "sciencey" or "scientif-ish." No one term floated to the top as a succinct way to convey the meaning that claimants were mimicking science, especially when the perpetrators of the ruse may be sincere but misinformed.

One day, while working on the idea of "sham inquiry" as a description of what ghost hunters really do (work backwards from conclusion to evidence), I came across the word "scientifical." I don't remember how. Perhaps it popped into my head because it was the word that sounded just as silly as these weekend investigators looked to an actual scientist. It was not widely used although it existed in the Urban Dictionary:

> A term used to describe a situation when someone has mixed
> up or mispronounced words. It is so used because it is such a

word itself. It is normally used to point out the persons [*sic*] blunder.

And also,

A way to make yourself sound intelligent when you have no idea what you are talking about.

These definitions certainly resonated with me in terms of what I found when looking at amateur paranormal investigation groups. So I used it. Being *scientifical* means hijacking the authority of science to sound credible and believable by misappropriating the terms, methods, and imagery.

Acting scientifical reflects a desire to be included within the scientific realm as opposed to excluded and ridiculed. This semblance is convincing to the non-science public where real-life experience can be valued more highly than academic credentials.

Everyone wants science on their side. If you can't get that to legitimately happen, it's not too difficult to bluff by manufacturing a facsimile. You fool some of the people a lot of the time. Those who play at this also fool themselves. They fail at obtaining useful, reliable knowledge about the natural world. Still, they are certain of their ways—using their *scientifical* methods, telling the public how serious and important their work is, and succeeding at converting some nonbelievers that there is something to it. That's dangerous and should be challenged.

Periodical and Internet Sources Bibliography

The following articles have been selected to supplement the diverse views presented in this chapter.

Soren Bowie	"Why 'Psychics' Need to Stop Pretending They Can Solve Crimes," Cracked.com, July 11, 2011.
Bonnie Cleaver	"Medium Frequency," *Good Health*, December 1, 2010.
Paul Desormeaux	"Cool Careers for Dummies: Psychic Detective," *Skeptical Inquirer*, March–April 2008.
Lucy Odling-Smee	"The Lab That Asked the Wrong Questions," *Nature*, March 2007.
Stephanie Pappas	"Get Kraken: Why Scientists Should Study Sea Monsters," *LiveScience*, July 6, 2011.
Danny Penman	"Mediums Really Do Talk to the Dead Claim Top Scientists," *NewsMonster*.
Marianne Power	"Can We All Learn to Be Psychic?," *Daily Mail*, May 27, 2012.
Benjamin Radford	"Texas Mass Grave Hoax: Do Police Actually Hire Psychics?," *Christian Science Monitor*, June 8, 2011.
Williams Ringer	"Demonology and the Paranormal Pandemic," *Paranormal Journal*, January 2010.
Michael Shermer	"A Skeptic's Review of Telephoning the Dead," *Scientific American*, January 2009.

For Further Discussion

Chapter 1

1. *Health and Medicine Week* reports that scientific research has not yielded proof for paranormal activity. Winston Wu, on the other hand, maintains that such proof exists and is ignored by mainstream science. In your view, which viewpoint offers the most persuasive argument? Why or why not?

2. Tim Weisberg maintains that physics supports the evidence of ghosts because the energy from human bodies cannot be destroyed. Do you agree or disagree with Weisberg? Why or why not?

3. The viewpoints by Lee Speigel and James Oberg both refer to a book by Leslie Kean, *UFOs: Generals, Pilots and Government Officials Go on the Record*. In your opinion, are military personnel, pilots, or elected officials credible witnesses of UFOs? Cite examples from both viewpoints to explain your response.

4. Melissa Burkley presents findings from several studies that indicate the possibility of psi phenomena. In your view, is the evidence that she provides strong enough to prove the ability to anticipate future events? Why or why not?

Chapter 2

1. Sharon Begley contends that when normal brain functions are intensified, ordinary stimuli can be misinterpreted as ghosts and psychic phenomena. In your opinion, does Begley's science-based position provide a satisfactory explanation for beliefs in the paranormal? Why or why not?

2. Robert Roy Britt states that some research indicates that religiosity can promote belief in the paranormal. Do you believe that being religious is more or less likely to encourage such beliefs? Cite examples from the viewpoint and your personal experience to support your answer.

3. Deonna Kelli Sayed says that paranormal reality shows have cultural meaning and reflect Americans coping with the terrorist attacks of 9/11. Do you agree or disagree with Sayed? Why or why not?

Chapter 3

1. As a psychic detective, Noreen Renier advises that she is not 100 percent accurate in her interpretations or equally successful in every case. In your opinion, does Renier's statement place her abilities under skepticism? Why or why not?

2. Julie Beischel states that mediums provide therapeutic value to grieving individuals while James Randi believes that mediums are charlatans akin to circus performers who may do more harm than good. Who do you think presents the more persuasive evidence? Does Beischel successfully counter Randi's position? Why or why not?

3. Jack Porter suggests that a paranormal investigator's lack of a doctorate or master's degree does not necessarily make his or her research illegitimate. How does his reasoning compare to Sharon Hill's position that the field is not scientific? Use examples from the viewpoints to explain your response.

Organizations to Contact

The editors have compiled the following list of organizations con-cerned with the issues debated in this book. The descriptions are derived from materials provided by the organizations. All have publications or information available for interested readers. The list was compiled on the date of publication of the present vol-ume; names, addresses, phone and fax numbers, and e-mail and Internet addresses may change. Be aware that many organizations take several weeks or longer to respond to inquiries, so allow as much time as possible.

British UFO Research Association (BUFORA)
PO Box 241, Business House
Herts, UK SG6 9AJ
44 08445 674 694
e-mail: enquiries@bufora.org.uk
website: www.bufora.org.uk

BUFORA works with other organizations that share a similar ethos and approach to investigations and research on UFOs. It seeks the facts through a scientific and factually evaluative ap-proach, and its team of investigators are required to pass a thor-ough course in all types of sightings. Along with accepting UFO eyewitness submissions online, the BUFORA website provides ar-ticles, news, and information on UFO investigations and research.

Committee for Skeptical Inquiry (CSI)
PO Box 703
Amherst, NY 14226
(716) 636-1425
website: www.csicop.org

A nonprofit scientific and educational organization established in 1976, CSI focuses on promoting scientific inquiry, critical inves-tigation, and the use of reason in examining controversial and extraordinary claims. Founding members include scientists, academics, and science writers such as Carl Sagan, Isaac Asimov, and James Randi. CSI publishes a bimonthly journal, *Skeptical Inquiry*, and the quarterly newsletter *Skeptical Briefs*. Articles, news, and other information on the paranormal is offered on its website.

International Cryptozoology Museum
PO Box 4311
Portland, ME 04101
e-mail: lcoleman@maine.rr.com
website: http://cryptozoologymuseum.com

Established in 2003, the International Cryptozoology Museum is the only one of its kind in the world. The museum contains more than two thousand pieces on cryptids, including various types of evidence, cultural artifacts, paraphernalia, and cryptozoology-inspired artwork. Its website provides information about the museum and its exhibitions.

International Paranormal Investigators (IPI)
website: www.ipi-radio.info

The IPI is a project serving paranormal investigators, whether seasoned or beginners to the field. Founded in 2006, the organization offers networking facilities to further enhance field communication. The IPI website provides a Starters Guide for investigators as well as articles and a discussion forum.

James Randi Educational Foundation (JREF)
7095 Hollywood Boulevard, No. 1170
Los Angeles, CA 90028
(703) 226-3780 • fax: (703) 226-3781
website: www.randi.org

Established by magician and skeptic James Randi, the JREF's mission is to promote critical thinking by reaching out to the public and media with information about common paranormal and supernatural ideas. The JREF offers a still-unclaimed million-dollar reward for anyone who can produce evidence of paranormal abilities under controlled conditions. Through scholarships, workshops, and innovative resources for educators, the foundation works to inspire an investigative spirit in a new generation of critical thinkers. E-books, podcasts, and a forum can be found on its website.

Parapsychological Association (PA)
PO Box 24173
Columbus, OH 43224
(202) 318-2364
website: www.parapsych.org

The PA is an international professional organization of scientists and scholars engaged in the study of psi (or "psychic") experiences, such as telepathy, clairvoyance, psychokinesis, psychic healing, and precognition. Its primary objective is to achieve a scientific understanding of these experiences. The PA offers news, a blog, and videos on its website.

Paranormal Research Society (PRS)
PO Box 403
State College, PA 16801
e-mail: society@the-prs.org
website: http://paranormalresearchsociety.org

Once a student organization at the University of Pennsylvania, the PRS gained national attention as the cast of the reality television show *Paranormal State*, which documented the group as it investigated reportedly haunted and paranormally active locations. Currently, the PRS offers investigative services for selected case submissions as well as resources for those who are haunted.

Scientific Committee to Evaluate PseudoSkeptical Criticism of the Paranormal (SCEPCOP)
e-mail: scepcop@debunkingskeptics.com
website: www.debunkingskeptics.com

SCEPCOP is a coalition of researchers, investigators, writers, intellectuals, and freethinkers advocating proper application of the scientific method, objectivity, and unbiased open inquiry toward all paranormal and unconventional data. Its website offers a discussion forum, videos, and articles as well as a list of books and information on skepticism and paranormal phenomenon.

The Skeptics Society

PO Box 338
Altadena, CA 91001
(626) 794-3119 • fax: (626) 794-1301
e-mail: skepticssociety@skeptic.com
website: www.skeptic.com

The Skeptics Society is a scientific and educational organization of scientists, scholars, investigative journalists, historians, professors, and teachers. Its mission is to investigate and provide a sound scientific viewpoint on claims of the paranormal, pseudoscience, fringe groups, and cults. The Skeptics Society publishes the magazines *Skeptic* and *Junior Skeptic* and offers podcasts, an electronic newsletter, and a forum on its website.

Windbridge Institute for Applied Research in Human Potential

1517 N. Wilmot Road, #254
Tucson, AZ 85712
e-mail: info@windbridge.org
website: www.windbridge.org

An independent research organization of a community of scientists, the Windbridge Institute investigates the capabilities of human bodies, minds, and spirits and attempts to determine how the resulting information can best serve all living things. The institute's website provides information on its research and peer-reviewed research papers, articles, and other materials.

Bibliography of Books

John B. Alexander

UFOs: Myths, Conspiracies, and Realities. New York: Thomas Dunne Books, 2011.

Christopher D. Bader, F. Carson Mencken, and Joseph O. Baker

Paranormal America: Ghost Encounters, UFO Sightings, Bigfoot Hunts, and Other Curiosities in Religion and Culture. New York: New York University Press, 2010.

Chris Carter

Science and Psychic Phenomena: The Fall of the House of Skeptics. Rochester, VT: Inner Traditions, 2012.

Richard M. Dolan and Bryce Zabel

A.D., After Disclosure: When the Government Finally Reveals the Truth About Alien Contact. Pompton Plains, NJ: New Page Books, 2012.

Nancy Du Tertre

Psychic Intuition: Everything You Ever Wanted to Ask But Were Afraid to Know. Pompton Plains, NJ: New Page Books, 2012.

Josh Gates

Destination Truth: Memoirs of a Monster Hunter. New York: Gallery Books, 2011.

Erich Goode

The Paranormal: Who Believes, Why They Believe, and Why It Matters. Amherst, NY: Prometheus Books, 2012.

Matthew Holm and Jonathan Follett — *Gray Highway: An American UFO Journey.* Hudson, NY: Toadspittle Hill, 2006.

Stacy Horn — *Unbelievable: Investigations into Ghosts, Poltergeists, Telepathy, and Other Unseen Phenomena from the Duke Parapsychology Laboratory.* New York: Ecco, 2009.

Mitch Horowitz — *Occult America: The Secret History of How Mysticism Shaped Our Nation.* New York: Bantam, 2009.

Donna M. Jackson — *Phenomena: Secret of the Senses.* New York: Little, Brown and Company, 2008.

Gary Jansen — *Holy Ghosts, or, How a (Not So) Good Catholic Boy Became a Believer in Things That Go Bump in the Night.* New York: J.P. Tarcher/Penguin, 2010.

John B. Kachuba — *Ghosthunters: On the Trail of Mediums, Dowsers, Spirit Seekers, and Other Investigators of America's Paranormal World.* Franklin Lakes, NJ: New Page Books, 2007.

Marc Kaufman — *First Contact: Scientific Breakthroughs in the Hunt for Life Beyond Earth.* New York: Simon & Schuster, 2011.

Jeffrey J. Kripal — *Authors of the Impossible: The Paranormal and the Sacred.* Chicago, IL: University of Chicago Press, 2010.

Stanley Krippner and Harris L. Friedman, eds. — *Debating Psychic Experience: Human Potential or Human Illusion?* Santa Barbara, CA: Praeger, 2010.

Paul Kurtz and John R. Shook, ed. — *Exuberant Skepticism.* Amherst, NY: Prometheus Books, 2010.

Jeffrey Long and Paul Perry — *Evidence of the Afterlife: The Science of Near-Death Experiences.* New York: HarperOne, 2010.

Raymond Moody and Paul Perry — *Paranormal: My Life in Pursuit of the Afterlife.* New York: HarperOne, 2012.

W. Scott Poole — *Monsters in America: Our Historical Obsessions with the Hideous and the Haunting.* Waco, TX: Baylor University Press, 2011.

Diane Hennacy Powell — *The ESP Enigma.* New York: Walker Books, 2008.

Kevin D. Randle — *Crash: When UFOs Fall from the Sky: A History of Famous Incidents, Conspiracies, and Cover-Ups.* Franklin Lakes, NJ: New Page Books, 2010.

Nick Redfern   *The Real Men in Black: Evidence, Famous Cases, and True Stories of These Mysterious Men and Their Connection to UFO Phenomena.* Pompton Plains, NJ: New Page Books, 2011.

Michael Shermer   *The Believing Brain: From Ghosts and Gods to Politics and Conspiracies—How We Construct Beliefs and Reinforce Them as Truths.* New York: Times Books, 2011.

Jonathan C. Smith   *Pseudoscience and Extraordinary Claims of the Paranormal: A Critical Thinker's Toolkit.* Malden, MA: Wiley-Blackwell, 2010.

Rory Storm   *Monster Hunt: The Guide to Cryptozoology.* New York: Sterling Publishing, 2008.

Russell Targ   *The Reality of ESP: A Physicist's Proof of Psychic Abilities.* Wheaton, IL: Quest Books, 2012.

Charles T. Tart   *The End of Materialism: How Evidence of the Paranormal Is Bringing Science and Spirit Together.* Oakland, CA: New Harbinger Publications/Noetic Books, 2009.

Pim van Lommel   *Consciousness Beyond Life: The Science of the Near-Death Experience.* New York: HarperOne, 2010.

Richard Wiseman   *Paranormality: Why We See What Isn't There*. London, UK: Pan MacMillan, 2011.

Index

CPSIA information can be obtained
at www.ICGtesting.com
Printed in the USA
FFOW030853120213
861FF